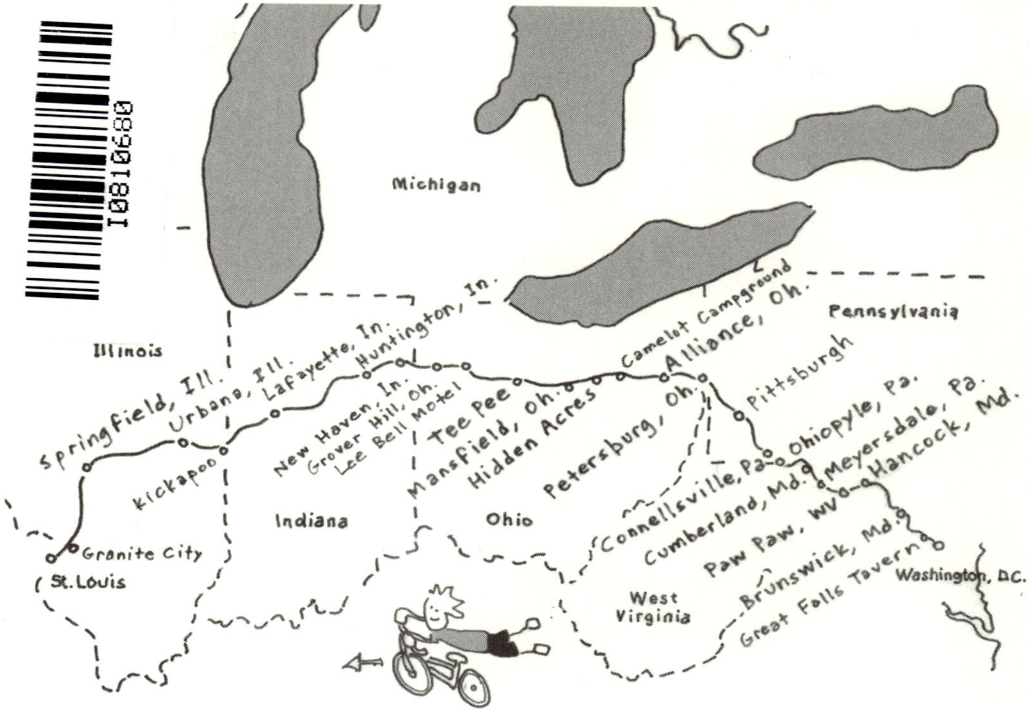
Michigan
Illinois
Pennsylvania
Indiana
Ohio
West Virginia
Springfield, Ill.
Urbana, Ill.
Lafayette, In.
Huntington, In.
Kickapoo
New Haven, In.
Grover Hill, Oh.
Lee Bell Motel
Tee Pee
Mansfield, Oh.
Hidden Acres
Camelot Campground
Alliance, Oh.
Petersburg, Oh.
Pittsburgh
Connellsville, Pa.
Ohiopyle, Pa.
Cumberland, Md.
Meyersdale, Pa.
Hancock, Md.
Paw Paw, WV
Brunswick, Md.
Great Falls Tavern
Washington, D.C.
Granite City
St. Louis

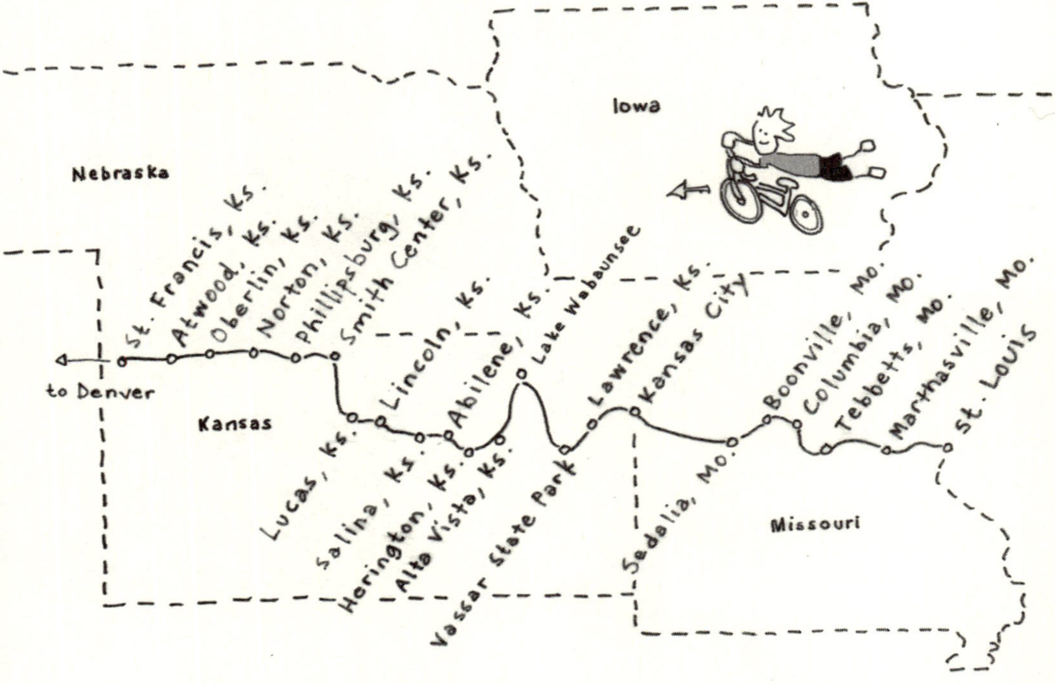
Nebraska
Iowa
Kansas
Missouri
to Denver
St. Francis, Ks.
Atwood, Ks.
Oberlin, Ks.
Norton, Ks.
Phillipsburg, Ks.
Smith Center, Ks.
Lucas, Ks.
Lincoln, Ks.
Salina, Ks.
Abilene, Ks.
Herington, Ks.
Alta Vista, Ks.
Lake Wabaunsee
Vassar State Park
Lawrence, Ks.
Kansas City
Sedalia, Mo.
Boonville, Mo.
Columbia, Mo.
Tebbetts, Mo.
Marthasville, Mo.
St. Louis

DETROIT
JULY, 2006

I SPENT A COUPLE YEARS MAKING A DOCUMENTARY MOVIE ABOUT ACTIVISTS WHO WORK ALONG THE U.S.-MEXICO BORDER. LOTS OF UNDOCUMENTED IMMIGRANTS FROM MEXICO HAVE DIED OF EXPOSURE WHILE TRYING TO CROSS INTO THE U.S., SO THESE ACTIVISTS SETUP WATER STATIONS OUT IN THE DESERT. AFTER I FINISH THE MOVIE, I GOT THE IDEA TO RIDE MY BIKE FROM THE EAST COAST TO THE WEST COAST AND TO SHOW MY MOVIE ALONG THE WAY. I GAVE THE PROJECT A NAME: THE PEDAL POWERED MOVIE TOUR. I ASKED SOME FRIENDS TO COME ALONG. I TOLD

THEM IT'LL BE FUN. I DIDN'T TELL THEM THAT I WAS TERRIFIED TO DO A TRIP LIKE THIS ALONE. SOME FRIENDS SAY IT SOUNDS LIKE A GREAT IDEA BUT THEY CAN'T COME SOME FRIENDS SAY IT SOUNDS CRAZY. BUT THEN I EMAIL LJR AND SHE SAYS SHE'LL DO IT, AND THAT SETTLES IT.

I SPEND JULY IN DETROIT, TOILING IN MY APARTMENT LIKE SOME GHETTO MERIWETHER LEWIS, PIECING TOGETHER A BIKE ROUTE FROM AN ASSORTMENT OF HIGHWAY MAPS, WEBSITES, AND CHAT ROOMS MODERATED BY BIKE FANATICS. SOMETIMES IT'S EASY. GETTING OUT OF D.C., FOR INSTANCE THERE'S A BIKE TRAIL THAT FOLLOWS THE OLD CHESAPEAKE

AND OHIO CANAL. FOR 185 MILES, YOU RIDE UNDER BIG TREES AND FOLLOW THE POTOMAC RIVER ALL THE WAY TO CUMBERLAND, MARYLAND. SOMETIMES IT'S HARD. PITTSBURGH IS HARD. AS FAR AS I CAN TELL, THERE'S NO WAY TO GET INTO THE CITY THAT DOESN'T INVOLVE A HALF-MILE TUNNEL OR A TWISTY HIGHWAY WITH NO SHOULDER. THE BEST THING TO DO IS AVOID THE PLACE ALTOGETHER, BUT THAT'S WHERE TED AND RENATO ARE GOING TO JOIN THE RIDE. I FOLLOW A MILLION THREADS ON A MILLION BIKE FORUMS, AND THEY ALL LEAD TO THE SAME UNHAPPY CONCLUSION: PITTSBURGH IS HARD. ALL THROUGH JULY, I WORRY ABOUT PITTSBURGH.

08/02/06

LJR AND I RENDEZVOUS AT HER FRIEND'S PLACE IN BETHESDA. NEITHER OF US HAS GONE ON A LONG RIDE LIKE THIS BEFORE. IN FACT, NEITHER OF US HAS RIDDEN A BIKE WITH MORE THAN THREE SPEEDS BEFORE. WE COMPARE OUR STUFF. LJR IS RIDING A BRIDGESTONE HYBRID THAT HER FRIEND GAVE HER. I BOUGHT A TREK 520 OFF CRAIGSLIST FROM A GUY IN SEATTLE. I ALSO SHELLED OUT FOR A COUPLE ORTLIEB PANNIERS BECAUSE EVERY BIKER IN THE WORLD RECOMMENDED THE THINGS; AND A BIKE SEAT WITH A SLIT DOWN THE CENTER FOR PERINEAL COMFORT, THOUGH AT THIS POINT, I DON'T HAVE A CLUE ABOUT MY

PERINEUM OR ITS COMFORT. LJR PULLS OUT A COUPLE PAIRS OF SPANDEX BIKING SHORTS. "YOU'VE GOT A PAIR, RIGHT?" I SHAKE MY HEAD. "OKAY, TRY THESE ON." I LOOK AT THE SHORTS. THEY'RE MADE OUT OF SOME STRETCHY SPACE-AGED FABRIC AND THEY'RE PADDED ON THE BUTT. I'VE ALWAYS RIDDEN JUNKER BIKES IN JUNKY CLOTHES, AND THESE SKINTIGHT BIKE SHORTS ARE A LINE I'M RELUCTANT TO CROSS. I TRY THEM ON. IT'S A WEIRD FEELING: PART BONDAGE GEAR, PART ADULT DIAPER. I FEEL STUPID AND JUST A TINY BIT SEXY. WHEN I FIGURE OUT I CAN WEAR THE THINGS UNDER MY CUT-OFFS, I ACCEPT THE GIFT. A MILLION MILES LATER, I ADMIT TO LJR

THAT I COULD NEVER HAVE GOTTEN VERY FAR WITHOUT THOSE SHORTS.

THE PLAN, AT FIRST, IS TO RIDE CLEAR ACROSS THE COUNTRY, FROM D.C. TO S.F. TROUBLE IS, IT'S ALREADY AUGUST AND BY MY CALCULATIONS, WE WON'T GET TO COLORADO TILL OCTOBER. CYCLIST DUDES I TALK TO WARN ME DARKLY ABOUT BLIZZARDS IN THE ROCKIES AND SNOW IN THE SIERRAS. THE DONNER PARTY COMES UP MORE THAN ONCE. SO WE CHANGE OUR PLANS. WE'LL AIM FOR DENVER.

08/03/06

I INSIST THAT WE START THE RIDE AT THE LINCOLN MEMORIAL, EVEN THOUGH IT'LL MEAN BACKTRACKING. IT'S AN ATTEMPT

TO GIVE THE RIDE A LITTLE SYMBOLISM.

"OF WHAT?" LJR WANTS TO KNOW. "THE CIVIL WAR? THE PRESERVATION OF THE UNION?"

I FINALLY ADMIT THAT IT JUST SOUNDS BETTER THAN SAYING WE STARTED FROM BETHESDA.

WE FIND THE BIKE TRAIL WITHOUT MUCH TROUBLE: THE C&O TRAIL, THAT FOLLOWS THE OLD CHESAPEAKE AND OHIO CANAL. IN THE OLD DAYS, MULES WOULD WALK ALONG THE TRAIL PULLING BARGES BETWEEN D.C. AND CUMBERLAND, MD. NOWADAYS, IT'S MOSTLY CIVIL SERVANTS ON HYBRID BIKES OUT ON A DAY TRIP.

15 MILES OUT, WE REACH THE GREAT FALLS TAVERN. BACK IN THE CANAL DAYS, YOU COULD GET A BITE HERE AND STAY THE NIGHT. NOW IT'S A VISITOR'S CENTER THAT'S CLOSED WHEN WE ROLL UP. WE EAT A FEW POWERBARS FROM LJR'S LARGE AND DIVERSE STASH (COOKIES & CREAM IS OKAY, BUT I'M NOT SURE WHAT HORRIBLE FLAVOR LABORATORY MISHAP RESULTED IN THE BANANA) AND WATCH AS THE TOTALLY EMPTY LITTLE CAMPGROUND NEXT TO THE TAVERN FADES INTO DARKNESS.

"I GUESS WE SHOULD PITCH THE TENTS," I SUGGEST.

"YEAH," LJR AGREES.

NO SOONER HAVE I SPOKEN THAN A CAR ROLLS SLOWLY INTO THE EMPTY PARKING LOT, CATCHES US IN ITS HEADLIGHTS, PAUSES, THEN ROLLS SLOWLY AWAY. LJR AND I QUIETLY CONSIDER THIS NEW DEVELOPMENT.

"I WONDER IF WE CAN SLEEP INSIDE THE TAVERN?" LJR SAYS.

"YEAH," I SAY.

WE STASH OUR BIKES BEHIND A COMPOST PILE IN THE TAVERN'S GARDEN AND TRY THE DOORS. THE PLACE IS LOCKED UP TIGHT. THEN WE NOTICE A LITTLE PORCH UP ON THE SECOND FLOOR. LJR SHIMMIES

UP A WOODEN SUPPORT POST. I TOSS OUR SLEEPING BAGS TO HER, THEN SHE PULLS ME UP. WE'RE NOT EXACTLY INVISIBLE UP THERE, BUT IT'S DARK AND WHEN WE'RE LYING DOWN, WE FIGURE WE'D BE HARD TO SPOT. EVEN SO, I CAN'T SLEEP. I LIE THERE, LISTENING TO THE SOUNDS OF THE NIGHT. THERE'S THE SLOSH OF THE RIVER, AND THE BUZZ OF THE CRICKETS, AND NOW AND THEN, THE LOW RUMBLE OF A CAR DRIVING SLOWLY THROUGH THE EMPTY PARKING LOT.

08/05/06

WE STOP AT THE BRUNSWICK FAMILY CAMPGROUND FOR THE

NIGHT. MY BUTT HURTS

"IT'D BE WORSE IF YOU WEREN'T WEARING THE BIKE SHORTS," LJR ASSURES ME.

THE CAMPGROUND MANAGER LIVES IN A BEAT-UP TRAILER. I FILL OUT A REGISTRATION CARD WHILE THE MANAGER'S SHIRTLESS LITTLE BOY FRIES UP A PAN OF HAMBURGER HELPER AT THE STOVE. AS LJR AND I RIDE TO OUR CAMPSITE, THE MANAGER'S TWEEN-AGED DAUGHTER COMES RACING UP BEHIND US ON HER BIKE.

"I'M A PARK RANGER AND YOU HAVE TO WEAR A BIKE HELMET,"

SHE ANNOUNCES BOSSILY.
"BUT YOU'RE NOT WEARING A BIKE HELMET," I POINT OUT. THE KID IS SPEECHLESS FOR A MOMENT OR TWO. THEN SHE RECOVERS. "IT'S A RULE," SHE HISSES, THEN SPEEDS AWAY.

LJR AND I PITCH OUR TENTS UNDER TALL TREES FULL OF CICADAS. IT'S FULL SUMMER NOW. NO MORE OF THE RECKLESSNESS OF MAY, WHEN THE GRASS GROWS A MILE-A-MINUTE AND EVERY DAY ENDS WITH THE CRASH OF THUNDER. THOSE WERE SUMMER'S PARTY DAYS. ITS WILD YOUTH. NOW SUMMER HAS MELLOWED INTO THE SULTRY CALM OF ITS MIDDLE AGE. CHECKING ITSELF OUT IN THE MIRROR. LOOKING FOR SIGNS OF THINNING FOLIAGE OR YELLOWING

LEAVES.

WE'RE CAMPED OUT NEAR A RAIL YARD. ALL NIGHT LONG, RAIL CARS COUPLE AND UNCOUPLE. SOMETIMES, A BIG FREIGHT TRAIN LURCHES FORWARD. THEN THE RAIL CARS CRASH INTO EACH OTHER, ONE AFTER ANOTHER. — BOOM, BOOM, BOOM — LIKE A LONG STRING OF BLACK CATS POPPING ON THE FOURTH OF JULY.

08/06/06

EVERY SNACK IS AN ENERGY BAR. LJR HAS A SADDLE BAG FULL OF THEM: LUNA BARS, LARABARS, AND CLIF BARS. THE BARS COME IN DIFFERENT FLAVORS, BUT

THEY ALL TASTE THE SAME TO ME. I'M READING A BOOK BY THE BRITISH EXPLORER WILFRED THESIGER. HE WANDERED FOR YEARS THROUGH THE DESERTS OF THE ARABIAN PENINSULA. MOSTLY HE ATE DRIED DATES. AFTER A WHILE, HE COULD BARELY FORCE THE THINGS DOWN. I ALREADY FEEL THE SAME WAY ABOUT ENERGY BARS. LJR SAYS WE HAVE TO EAT THEM OR ELSE WE'LL "BONK," WHICH IS A TERM SHE PICKED UP FROM HER FRIEND THE BICYCLE RACER. I ASK HER WHAT IT MEANS TO BONK. SHE TELLS ME SHE ISN'T EXACTLY SURE, BUT IT'S BAD. FOR THE LAST COUPLE DAYS, WE HAVEN'T PASSED THROUGH ANY TOWNS, SO WE'VE BEEN LIVING ON ENERGY BARS. WHEN WE COME ACROSS A WAFFLE HOUSE IN WILLIAMSPORT, WE NEARLY LOSE OUR MINDS IN EXCITEMENT. LJR IS FROM

ATLANTA, SO SHE ORDERS AN ATLANTA-STYLE BREAKFAST: SCRAMBLED EGGS, GRITS, AND A LARGE COKE.

SOMEONE TELLS US THERE'S A GOOD PLACE TO STAY IN HANCOCK, MARYLAND. THE GUY WHO RUNS THE LOCAL BIKE SHOP BUILT A LITTLE BUNKHOUSE JUST OFF THE TRAIL. FOR 10 BUCKS, YOU CAN SIT AROUND HIS HOMEMADE FOUNTAIN SWATTING MOSQUITOES AND DRINKING YUENGLING BEER, AND YOU CAN CLEAN UP IN ONE OF THE PORTAPOTS HE'S CONVERTED INTO A SHOWER.

LJR AND I WALK INTO TOWN FOR DINNER. WE FIND A LOCAL JOINT CALLED WEAVER'S. I ORDER A SLICE OF CARAMEL NUT APPLE PIE FOR DESSERT. LJR

ORDERS THE COCONUT CREAM.

"HAH!" SAYS THE YOUNG WAITRESS, "I KNEW YOU'D ORDER THAT!" THE WAITRESS TELLS US SHE OFTEN KNOWS WHAT SOMEONE IS GOING TO ORDER. SHE FEELS IT IN HER BONES. SHE TELLS US SHE'S ALMOST ALWAYS RIGHT.

08/07/06

PAW PAW, WEST VIRGINIA ISN'T MUCH OF A TOWN. THE CONVENIENCE STORE IS CALLED THE LIBERTY GAS EXPRESS STOP: PICK-UP TRUCKS OUTSIDE, GUYS IN BLAZE ORANGE CAMO OVERALLS INSIDE. IT'S NOT THE KIND OF TOWN YOU'D EXPECT TO FIND A HOSTEL, BUT THERE IT IS: THE RED ROOSTER. WE RIDE UP TO THE FRONT DOOR. IT'S LOCKED. IN FACT, THE PLACE LOOKS LIKE IT'S SHUT DOWN.

WE'RE RIDING AWAY WHEN SOMEONE YELLS AT US FROM AROUND BACK. "HEY!" SAYS THE VOICE. THE GUY'S NAME IS BILLY. HE HAS A SHAVED HEAD AND A BUNCH OF TATTOOS. BILLY TELLS US THE HOSTEL HAS BEEN CLOSED FOR THE PAST COUPLE SUMMERS BECAUSE THE OWNER, J.D., HAS BEEN ON VACATION. "YOU'RE THE FIRST CUSTOMERS IN A REAL LONG TIME," BILLY TELLS US. I GIVE LJR A LOOK WHICH I HOPE TELEGRAPHS TO HER WHAT I'M THINKING, WHICH IS SOMETHING LIKE "LET'S GET THE FUCK OUT OF HERE BEFORE THIS SKINHEAD SENDS US ON THE SAME QUOTE-UNQUOTE VACATION THAT HE DISPATCHED J.D. ON!" BUT LJR IS FROM GEORGIA, SO, AS SHE'LL TELL ME LATER, SHE KNOWS A THING OR TWO ABOUT SKETCHY SKINHEADS. SHE ASKS BILLY HOW MUCH A ROOM

COSTS. IT'S CHEAP, SO WE STAY.

THE RED ROOSTER HAS A HOARDER AESTHETIC. IT'S FULL OF BIG PILES OF THINGS: VINTAGE VINYL RECORDS; COLLECTIBLE TOYS; COMMEMORATIVE PORCELAIN PLATES. THERE'S A HOLLOW-BODY GIBSON GUITAR LYING ON THE TOP BUNK OF THE BUNK BED IN OUR ROOM. BILLY DISAPPEARS FOR A WHILE, SO WE CREEP AROUND THE PLACE, PEEKING IN THE EMPTY ROOMS, READING OLD POSTCARDS FROM PREVIOUS GUESTS THAT ARE TACKED TO THE WALL. IT SEEMS LIKE WE'RE THE FIRST GUESTS IN A VERY LONG TIME.

IN THE MORNING, LJR TELLS ME WHAT HAPPENED AFTER I WENT TO BED. LJR WENT TO THE LAUNDRY ROOM TO DO SOME LAUNDRY. THEN BILLY CAME BACK. HE WAS DRUNK.

HE STARTED TELLING LJR HIS LIFE STORY. HE USED to BE A METH HEAD. BUT THEN HIS BROTHER GOT CANCER AND NEEDED MONEY FOR THE TREATMENT, SO HE - BILLY - SET OFF ALONE ON A CROSS-COUNTRY BIKE RIDE TO RAISE CASH. THAT'S HOW HE WOUND UP IN PAW PAW AND STAYED AT THE RED ROOSTER. ALL THIS HAPPENED A FEW YEARS AGO. BUT RECENTLY, HE CAME BACK TO PAW PAW AND OFFERED TO MANAGE THE HOSTEL FOR J.D., WHO SEEMS TO HAVE LOST INTEREST IN THE PLACE. LJR TELLS ME SHE FELT SAD FOR THE GUY. SHE ALSO TELLS ME SHE KNOWS A THING OR TWO ABOUT SKETCHY SKINHEADS, SO WHEN SHE FINALLY GOT BACK TO OUR ROOM, SHE LOCKED THE DOOR.

IN THE MORNING, WE RIDE OVER TO THE LIBERTY GAS EXPRESS STOP. THE PLACE HAS A DELI COUNTER, SO WE ORDER A COUPLE VEGGIE SUBS FROM A HIGH SCHOOL GIRL NAMED KASEY. WE DON'T EXPECT MUCH — I MEAN, IT'S A DELI COUNTER IN A GAS STATION IN WEST VIRGINIA — BUT KASEY MAKES A MEAN VEGGIE SUB. WHILE SHE'S WORKING, SHE TELLS US ABOUT THE GREAT FLOOD OF 1985, WHEN THE POTOMAC TOPPED ITS BANKS AND WIPED OUT THE TRAILER PARK. WE TELL HER WE MET BILLY AT THE RED ROOSTER, AND SHE SMILES TO HERSELF LIKE SHE'S GOT A LOT TO SAY ON THE SUBJECT.

"SOME PEOPLE COME TO PAW PAW," KASEY SAYS, "AND THEY NEVER LEAVE."

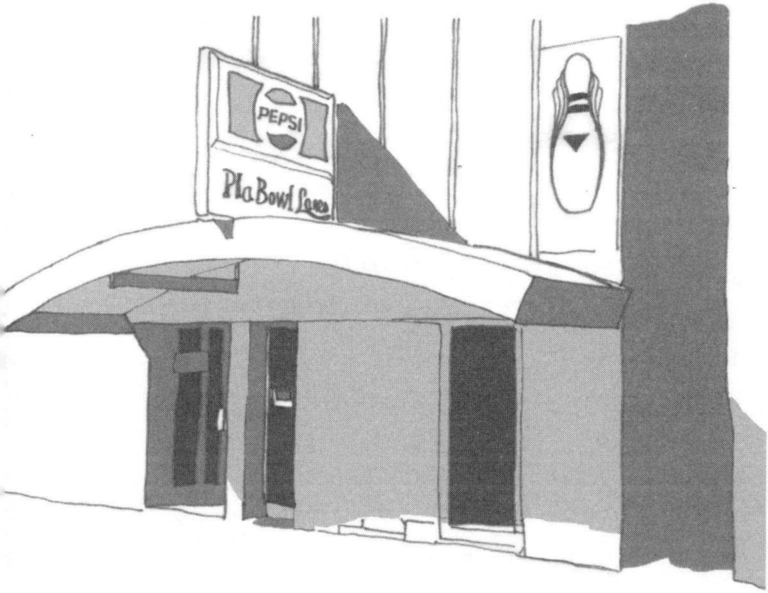
PEPSI
Pla Bowl

08/09/06

CUMBERLAND, MARYLAND IS ALL RED BRICK AND ROW HOUSES, AN OLD CANAL TOWN THAT'S SEEN BETTER DAYS. I LIKE HOW PEOPLE TALK HERE, SOFT AND WITH A LITTLE TWANG, AN EAST COAST ACCENT WITH A SOUTHERN DRAWL. AN ACCENT THAT HOVERS SOMEWHERE BETWEEN NORTH AND SOUTH, LIKE MARYLAND ITSELF, SITTING JUST BELOW THE MASON-DIXON LINE.

WE SPEND THE NIGHT IN AN EMPTY FIELD ACROSS THE STREET FROM THE YMCA. WE WALK OVER TO THE Y AND ASK THE GIRL AT THE FRONT DESK WHAT HER FAVORITE PIZZA PLACE IS. HARTLEY'S, SHE TELLS US. SO WE CALL HARTLEY'S AND ORDER A VEGAN PIZZA. THE PIZZA GUY DELIVERS IT RIGHT TO OUR TENT LIKE HE DOES THAT ALL

THE TIME.

08/10/06

THE NICE THING ABOUT CAMPING OUT IN A VACANT LOT IN A PRETTY BIG TOWN IS THAT WE CAN GET A DECENT COFFEE AT THE LOCAL COFFEE PLACE IN THE MORNING. AN OLD MAN WALKS OVER WHILE WE'RE LOCKING UP THE BIKES.

"WHERE YA HEADED?" HE ASKS.

"PITTSBURGH," WE TELL HIM.

HE SMILES AND PATS ME ON THE BACK.

"GOOD LUCK IN THE NARROWS," HE SAYS.

MY HEART SINKS. THE NARROWS.

CUMBERLAND IS WHERE THE C&O TRAIL ENDS AND THE ALLEGHENY TRAIL BEGINS, AND WHERE WE SWITCH FROM A TRAIL THAT

PARALLELS AN ABANDONED CANAL TO A TRAIL THAT FOLLOWS AN ABANDONED RAILROAD. TO GET FROM ONE TO THE OTHER, WE HAVE TO RIDE THROUGH THE NARROWS. SINCE MAPPING OUT THE TRIP BACK IN DETROIT, I'VE BEEN DREADING IT. A BOTTLENECK THROUGH WILLS MOUNTAIN THAT EVERYTHING SQUEEZES THROUGH: WILLS CREEK, AND A BUNCH OF BUSY RAILROAD TRACKS, AND A SPEEDY HIGHWAY WITH NO SHOULDER. THERE'S NO WAY AROUND IT. LJR AND I FIND HIGHWAY 40 AND START RIDING. IT'S OKAY AT FIRST. BUT THEN THE ROAD NARROWS, AND THE SHOULDER DISAPPEARS, AND PRETTY SOON WE'RE TEETERING ON THE CRUMBLING WHITE LINE THAT'S THE ONLY THING SEPARATING THE BIG RIGS SCREAMING BY ON OUR LEFT FROM THE STEEP

DROP INTO THE CREEK ON OUR RIGHT.

AND THEN WE'RE OUT. JUST LIKE THAT. I'M A LITTLE DISAPPOINTED. AFTER SO MANY WEEKS OF WORRYING ABOUT IT, IT SEEMS LIKE THE NARROWS SHOULD HAVE BEEN MORE TERRIFYING.

WE FOLLOW WOODCOCK HOLLOW ROAD TO THE ALLEGHENY TRAIL TRAILHEAD. IT'S A STEEP CLIMB.

"YOU'RE ALMOST AT THE TOP!" AN OLD LADY CALLS TO US FROM HER FRONT PORCH.

"THANKS," WE GASP BACK.

"HOW FAR ARE Y'ALL RIDING?" SHE ASKS.

"PITTSBURGH."

"THAT'S NICE."

WE'RE RIDING SO SLOW THAT OUR CONVERSATION WITH THIS LADY ENDS

BEFORE WE'VE GOTTEN HALFWAY PAST HER HOUSE, WHICH LEAVES TIME FOR SEVERAL MOMENTS OF AWKWARD SILENCE BEFORE WE'RE FINALLY CLEAR OF HER FRONT YARD.

THE FIRST PART OF THE TRAIL PARALLELS THE WESTERN MARYLAND SCENIC RAILWAY TRACKS. A GROUP DOWN IN CUMBERLAND RUNS SIGHT-SEEING TRAINS OVER TO FROSTBURG. BUT WHO CARES ABOUT TRAINS? WE'RE ON OUR BIKES, PEDALING OVER THE ALLEGHENYS, SNEAKING THROUGH ABANDONED RAILROAD TUNNELS AND CLATTERING OVER ABANDONED RAILROAD TRESTLES, SECRET AND STEALTHY, LIKE OUTLAWS ON THE RUN.

WE CROSS INTO PENNSYLVANIA WITHOUT EVEN KNOWING IT, AND ROLL INTO MEYERSDALE AT DINNER TIME. THERE'S A FLIER TACKED TO THE WALL AT THE OLD RAILROAD STATION

WITH THE PHONE NUMBER OF THE MEYERSDALE HOSTEL.

"JUST RIDE DOWN THE HILL," THE GUY ON THE PHONE TELLS ME, "I'LL MEET YOU THERE."

HALFWAY DOWN THE HILL THAT CUTS THROUGH TOWN, A CAR PULLS UP TO LJR AND ME.

"YOU LOOKIN' FOR THE HOSTEL?" A YOUNGISH GUY ASKS US.

"YEAH," WE SAY.

"FOLLOW ME," THE GUY SAYS. "I'M THE MAYOR."

WE FOLLOW THE MAYOR AT A SLOW, STATELY MAYORAL SPEED TO A BIG, HAUNTED-LOOKING PILE OF BRICKS THAT USED TO BE THE MEYERSDALE HIGH SCHOOL. THE SCHOOL SHUT DOWN YEARS AGO, BUT DURING THE SUMMER, THE TOWN LETS BIKE RIDERS SLEEP IN THE BASEMENT.

AFTER A FEW FORMALITIES, THE MAYOR TAKES OFF, LEAVING LJR AND ME ALONE IN THE ABANDONED BASEMENT OF THE ABANDONED HIGH SCHOOL. THE FOOTBALL TEAM'S LOCKER ROOM USED T BE DOWN HERE, BUT NOW THE LOCKERS HAVE BEEN REPLACED BY BUNK BEDS, AND AN OLD TV, AND A COFFEE TABLE WITH A FAKE HOUSE PLANT. TO GET TO THE TOILET, YOU HAVE TO PASS THROUGH THE SHOWERS, WHICH LOOK FAMILIAR BECAUSE I'VE SEEN THEM IN ABOUT A HALF-DOZEN 1980'S HORROR MOVIES: MILDEWY TILED WALLS, AND DOZENS OF SHOWER NOZZLES DRIPPING WATER, AND A FEW FLICKERING FLORESCENT TUBES IN THE CEILING. THERE'S A MUSKY SMELL, LIKE THE SMELL OF MOIST DIRT WHEN YOU'RE ON YOUR HANDS AND KNEES, DOWN CLOSE TO IT. I TAKE A

MOMENT TO CONSIDER THE SHOWER DRAIN, AND ALL THE STUFF THAT'S DRAINED DOWN IT. DECADES OF DRAINING AWAY THE STUFF THAT GETS SHOWERED OFF HIGH SCHOOL FOOTBALL TEAMS. "THE HORROR," I MUTTER TO MYSELF.

LATER, LJR AND I WALK BACK UP THE HILL LOOKING FOR DINNER. WE FIND A PIZZA PLACE THAT'S IN A SPACE THAT ONCE HOUSED A MUCH BIGGER BUSINESS — A DEPARTMENT STORE, MAYBE — AND IS SEVERAL SIZES TOO BIG FOR THE PIZZA PLACE. MAYBE IT'S THAT, OR MAYBE IT'S THE NOT-SO-FRIENDLY STARES FROM THE OTHER CUSTOMERS, BUT WE GET THE PIZZA AND A SIX-PACK TO GO. BACK AT THE HIGH SCHOOL, WE SIT ON THE LONG WOODEN BENCH

OUTSIDE THE PRINCIPAL'S OFFICE, EATING PIZZA AND DRINKING BEER AND FEELING LIKE A COUPLE DELINQUENTS ABOUT TO GET SUSPENDED.

08/11/06

IT'S PEAK SEASON IN OHIOPYLE, WHICH MEANS ALL THE FOOD IN TOWN IS OVERPRICED AND ALL THE KIDS ARE SMEARED WITH SUNSCREEN AND SOFT SERVE ICE CREAM. PEOPLE COME TO THIS RESORT TOWN TO RIDE THE RAPIDS ON THE YOUGHIGHENY RIVER. WE SPEND THE NIGHT IN THE WOODS, AND IN THE MORNING, WE HIKE OVER TO THE "NATURAL WATER SLIDE" WHICH IS ONE OF THE ONLY THINGS IN TOWN THAT'S FREE. THE WATER SLIDE IS A NARROW CHUTE THAT THE RIVER HAS CARVED OUT OF THE

BEDROCK. THE WAY IT WORKS IS YOU HIKE UPSTREAM TO THE TOP OF THE CHUTE AND, SETTING ASIDE YOUR SELF-PRESERVATION INSTINCTS AND BETTER JUDGEMENT, YOU SIT ON YOUR BUTT AND LET THE RIVER WHISK YOU AWAY. IF YOU'RE LUCKY, YOU WIND UP A FEW HUNDRED YARDS DOWNSTREAM WITHOUT A BLUNT HEAD INJURY AND STILL WEARING YOUR BATHING SUIT. NOT EVERYONE IS LUCKY.

"IT'S A WHITE TRASH WATER PARK," LJR OBSERVES.

I WANT NOTHING TO DO WITH THIS THING. BUT THEN LJR FASHIONS A HARNESS FOR MY GLASSES OUT OF ONE OF HER SHOE LACES, SO WHAT CAN I DO? I QUICKLY FIGURE OUT THAT WHAT'S 'NATURAL' ABOUT THE WATER SLIDE IS THE PAIN YOU FEEL

WHEN A RIVER SMASHES YOUR BODY INTO A BUNCH OF ROCKS. EVEN LJR AGREES THAT ONE RUN IS ENOUGH.

WE MAKE IT TO CONNELLSVILLE AS THE SUN IS SETTING. THE GREAT ALLEGHENY TRAIL RUNS RIGHT THROUGH THE MIDDLE OF TOWN ON ITS OWN DEDICATED BIKE STREET. IT'S NOT THE KIND OF AMENITY I EXPECT TO FIND IN A FADED OLD COAL TOWN IN WESTERN PENNSYLVANIA. AND MAYBE IT'S BECAUSE OF THAT, OR BECAUSE OF THE CICADAS CHATTERING IN THE TREES, OR THE LITTLE HOUSES WITH THEIR WINDOWS WIDE OPEN. MAYBE IT'S BECAUSE IT'S AUGUST, AND THE EVENING IS LIKE A SHOT OF SOMETHING THAT'S COOL AND CLEAR AND HIGH PROOF. WHATEVER IT IS, IT GIVES ME

GOOSEBUMPS. THE SWEET, SAD PERFECTION OF CONNELLSVILLE.

WE PITCH OUR TENTS BY THE RIVER, AND IN THE MORNING, WE CHECK EMAIL AT THE LIBRARY. THE TOWN IS FULL OF LEFTOVERS FROM A MORE PROSPEROUS PAST, AND THE LIBRARY IS NO EXCEPTION. THE REFERENCE LIBRARIAN TELLS US IT WAS BUILT IN 1903 IN THE ITALIANATE STYLE, BACK WHEN THE MINES WERE OPERATING AND THE TOWN WAS BOOMING. THE LIBRARIAN IS SITTING BEHIND A MASSIVE, ORNATELY CARVED DESK.

"SOMEONE OFFERED US A MILLION DOLLARS FOR IT BACK IN THE 1960'S," SHE TELLS US.

TO ITS UNDYING CREDIT, THE LIBRARY REFUSED THE OFFER. UPSTAIRS,

THERE'S AN OLD AUDITORIUM, WITH CREAKY WOODEN FLOORS AND A STAGE WITH RED VELVET CURTAINS. WILLIAM JENNINGS BRYAN SPOKE ON THAT STAGE ONCE. NOW THEY USE THE ROOM FOR STORAGE.

08/13/12

I OVERHEAR SOME CAMPER SAY THE PERSEIDS ARE OUT, SO I LIE AWAKE WITH MY TENT FLAP OPEN, WATCHING THE SKY FOR METEORS. IN THE MORNING, I'M NOT SURE IF I SAW SHOOTING STARS OR JUST DREAMT THEM: GREEN STREAKS IN THE SKY, LIKE SOME GALACTIC-SIZED HAND WAS TRYING TO STRIKE MATCHES AGAINST THE ATMOSPHERE.

LJR AND I RIDE IN SILENCE. MAYBE 10 DAYS OF HANGING OUT IN EVERY

SHAGGY CAMPGROUND AND CHEAP DINER BETWEEN D.C. AND PITTSBURGH IS MORE THAN TWO PEOPLE CAN BEAR.

ROSS RIDES DOWN FROM PITTSBURGH WITH A COUPLE FRIENDS AND MEETS LJR AND ME ABOUT 20 MILES SOUTH OF THE CITY. THEN WE ALL RIDE TOGETHER BACK TO McKEESPORT WHERE ROSS HAS PARKED HIS PICKUP TRUCK. BACK WHEN I WAS MAPPING OUT THE RIDE, THIS PART HAD ME STUMPED. THE GREAT ALLEGHENY TRAIL ENDS IN McKEESPORT (OR AT LEAST IT DID IN 2006), AND AFTER THAT, YOU'RE ON YOUR OWN. EVERYONE I EMAILED TOLD ME THE SAME THING: THE ONLY WAY TO GET FROM McKEESPORT TO PITTSBURGH IS TO RIDE ON A BIG, BUSY ROAD CALLED ROUTE 837. SOME NIGHTS, I'D DREAM I'D FINALLY FIGURED OUT A BYPASS ROUTE, ONLY

TO WAKE UP AND REALIZE I HADN'T. AT SOME POINT, I CAME UP WITH WHAT I THOUGHT WAS A SOLUTION, AN INSANELY COMPLICATED ROUTE THAT INVOLVED A FEW VERY STEEP HILLS, SOME TRESPASSING, AND CATCHING A RIDE ON A LIGHT RAIL. INSTEAD, WE TOSS OUR BIKES INTO ROSS' PICKUP AND WE SHOOT STRAIGHT INTO TOWN. IT'S A RELIEF, I GUESS, BUT WHERE'S THE GLORY? I VOW THAT I WON'T LEAVE THIS TOWN THE SAME WAY I ARRIVED, IN A DAMN CAR.

LJR AND I HANG OUT IN PITTSBURGH FOR A FEW DAYS WAITING FOR RENATO TO SHOW UP FROM MILWAUKEE AND TED TO DRIVE OUT FROM PHILLY. MEANWHILE, I CONSULT WITH ROSS ABOUT BIKE ROUTES OUT OF PITTSBURGH.

"HOW ABOUT ROUTE 51?" I ASK.

ROSS SHAKES HIS HEAD.

"THAT ROAD IS INFAMOUS. LOTS OF WRECKS."

"HOW ABOUT ROUTE 65?"

ROSS SHAKES HIS HEAD AGAIN.

"IF I HAD TO CHOOSE, I'D TAKE ROUTE 51."

"BUT YOU WOULDN'T RECOMMEND ROUTE 51?"

"CORRECT," ROSS SAYS.

)8/15/06

SHOW MY MOVIE ABOUT THE U.S.-MEXICO
ORDER AT THE LOCAL MOVIE MAKING
ENTER. BEFORE THE SCREENING, I
ELL LJR THAT I HOPE WE GET ONE
UDIENCE MEMBER FOR EVERY MILE
E BIKED FROM D.C. BUT WHEN IT'S
HOWTIME, ONLY A FEW PEOPLE ARE THERE.

AFTER THE SHOW, WE BIKE BACK TO JESSIE'S PLACE THROUGH EMPTY, LATE NIGHT STREETS. NEAR DOWNTOWN, A GIANT DUMPTRUCK PRACTICALLY RUNS US OFF THE ROAD. ROSS SHRUGS. "YOU CAN'T GET MAD," HE SAYS. I DON'T KNOW IF HE MEANS YOU CAN'T GET MAD AT PSYCHO DRIVERS BECAUSE, IF YOU DO, YOU'LL ALWAYS BE MAD; OR IF HE MEANS YOU CAN'T GET MAD BECAUSE WHENEVER A PITTSBURGH DRIVER DOESN'T KILL YOU, THEY'RE PRETTY MUCH DOING YOU A FAVOR.

08/16/06

RENATO'S TRAIN IS DUE AT 4AM. AT A QUARTER TILL, LJR AND I

PULL OURSELVES OUT OF OUR SLEEPING BAGS. IT'S ALL DOWNHILL TO THE AMTRAK STATION. WE SLUMP OVER OUR HANDLE BARS, HALF-ASLEEP, BLOWING THROUGH STOP LIGHTS AND PAST ALL THE CLOSED UP WAREHOUSES ON SMALLMAN STREET. AT THIS HOUR, NO ONE'S AROUND: JUST A COUPLE COPS, SOME HOMELESS GUYS, AND THE SLEEPLESS DEAD. RENATO GETS OFF THE TRAIN WEARING A TIGHT ORANGE CYCLING JERSEY AND SPANDEX SHORTS, LIKE HE'S COMING FROM MILWAUKEE BY WAY OF THE TOUR DE FRANCE.

WE SLEEP TILL THE AFTERNOON. WHEN WE WAKE UP, WE MAKE COFFEE AND LOOK AT THE MAPS.

AFTER AN HOUR OF LOOKING AT ROUTES, WE ALL AGREE THAT BIKING OUT OF PITTSBURGH IS IMPOSSIBLE. LATER, LJR AND RENATO GO TO A THRIFT STORE AROUND THE CORNER. WHILE THEY'RE THERE, THEY MEET A GIRL WHO JUST BIKED FROM PITTSBURGH ALL THE WAY TO COLORADO, AND WHO CLAIMS TO KNOW A WAY OUT OF TOWN. THEY CONVINCE HER TO COME BACK TO JESSIE'S APARTMENT TO SHOW US. WE'RE PRETTY EXCITED WHEN WE SIT DOWN IN FRONT OF THE MAPS AGAIN. THE GIRL POINTS TO ROUTE 51.

"BUT WE HEARD THAT ROAD IS PRETTY SCARY," I SAY.

SHE CONSIDERS THIS. THEN SHE NODS.

"YEAH, I GUESS IT IS. MAYBE YOU

SHOULD TAKE ROUTE 65."

"OUR FRIEND ROSS SAYS THAT ROAD IS EVEN WORSE," I SAY.

"HM," THE GIRL SAYS. "HE'S PROBABLY RIGHT."

"BUT WHAT ROAD DID YOU TAKE?" I ASK.

"ACTUALLY, I GOT A LIFT OUT OF TOWN FROM A FRIEND," SHE SAYS. SHE GIVES THE MAPS ANOTHER LOOK. "I GUESS IT'S PRETTY HARD TO BIKE OUT OF PITTSBURGH."

TED GETS TO TOWN LATER THAT NIGHT WITH HIS PAL MIKE. TED'S BIKE IS A TEN SPEED WITH A RUSTY CHAIN THAT HE BORROWED FROM A FRIEND. TED DOESN'T HAVE A TENT AND HE DIDN'T BRING PADDED BIKING SHORTS. IN THE DAYS AHEAD,

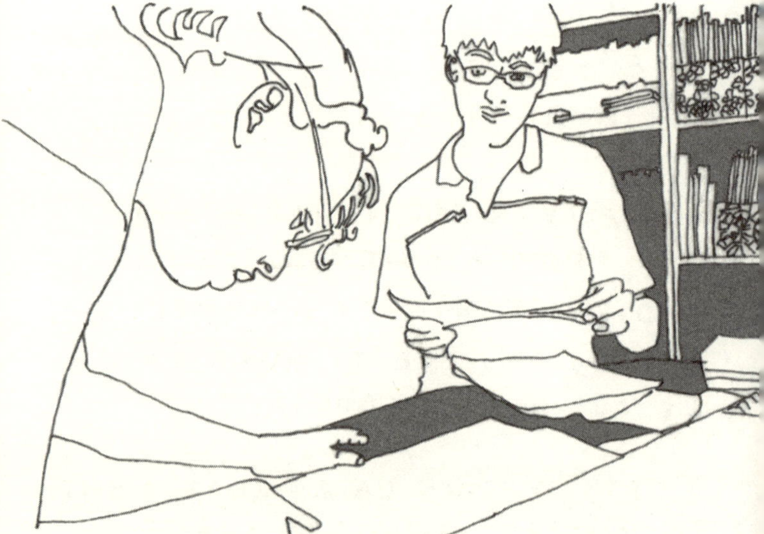

THESE SEEMINGLY INSIGNIFICANT DETAILS WILL BLOSSOM INTO A SAD, PAINFUL REALITY FOR TED.

THAT NIGHT, WE CRASH WITH SOME PUNK KIDS TED KNOWS. ONE OF THE KIDS, ANDY, TELLS US ABOUT THE NEIGHBORHOOD WE'RE IN, GARFIELD. IT USED TO BE A WORKING CLASS IRISH 'HOOD, BUT THEN CAME THE "URBAN RENEWAL" AND THE WHITE FLIGHT, AND BY THE 80'S, THE PLACE WAS DOWN ON ITS LUCK. ANDY TELLS US RIGHT NOW IS GARFIELD'S GOLDEN AGE — THAT MAGICAL MOMENT WHEN THE RENTS ARE STILL CHEAP AND THERE'S A VEGAN CAFE AROUND THE CORNER. THERE ARE PUNK HOUSES AND ART BIKES AND SOME NEW STOREFRONT GALLERIES.

LIKE ALL GOLDEN AGES, SOME DAY IT WILL END AND SOME OTHER AGE WILL BEGIN. THE CONDO AGE? THE OLD-BLACK-RESIDENTS-GET-PRICED OUT AGE? BUT FOR NOW, GARFIELD IS GREAT.

08/17/06

WE'VE FINALLY GOT A PLAN. LJR AND I CATCH THE 21A BUS TO CORAOPOLIS. SINCE THE RACK ON THE FRONT OF THE BUS ONLY HAS ROOM FOR TWO BIKES, TED AND RENATO HITCH A RIDE WITH MIKE. MIKE, BY THE WAY, WILL WIND UP JOINING THE RIDE IN ST. LOUIS, BUT MORE ABOUT THAT LATER. THE BUS LUMBERS ALONG ROUTE 51 AND MIKE FOLLOWS BEHIND. I PRETEND THAT THE WHINE OF THE

BUS ENGINE AS WE GRIND UP ONE HILL AFTER ANOTHER IS THE SOUND OF US REACHING ESCAPE VELOCITY AND FINALLY PULLING FREE OF PITTSBURGH'S SUPER STRONG GRAVITY. WE GET OFF THE BUS JUST PAST CORAOPOLIS, WEST OF THE CITY. WE FIGURE WE'RE HOME FREE NOW.

MIKE SNAPS A FEW PHOTOS AND WAVES GOODBYE, AND WE ROLL ONTO ROUTE 51. THERE ARE FOUR OF US NOW. RENATO, WHO WAS ON HIS COLLEGE CYCLING TEAM AND WHO WEARS SPECIAL SHOES THAT SNAP INTO HIS PEDALS, INSTRUCTS US TO RIDE IN A CLOSELY SPACED SINGLE FILE.

"IT'S CALLED A PELOTON," HE SHOUTS BACK TO US. "THAT'S THE FRENCH WORD FOR PACK."

WE DON'T LOOK LIKE A PACK, THOUGH. MORE LIKE A HERD. OR A GAGGLE.

RENATO ALSO TRIES TO DEMONSTRATE DRAFTING, WHICH IS WHEN YOU RIDE JUST INCHES AWAY FROM THE BIKE AHEAD OF YOU TO REDUCE WIND RESISTANCE. BUT AFTER WE CRASH INTO EACH OTHER A COUPLE TIMES, RENATO GIVES UP ON THE WHOLE DRAFTING THING.

THERE'S NO SHOULDER, BUT THE HIGHWAY HAS TWO LANES IN EACH DIRECTION, SO IT'S NOT SO BAD.

"IT'S NOT SO BAD!" I SHOUT BACK TO LJR. IN FACT, I'M FEELING PRETTY GOOD ABOUT OUR ESCAPE FROM PITTSBURGH. THIS FEELING LASTS FOR APPROXIMATELY ONE MILE. THEN THE CONSTRUCTION STARTS. THE TWO LANE HIGHWAY RAPIDLY NARROWS INTO A ONE LANE CHUTE, WITH A CONCRETE JERSEY BARRIER ON THE

LEFT AND A FOOT-HIGH CURB ON THE RIGHT.

"WHAT SHOULD WE DO?" I SHOUT TO RENATO.

"GO!" HE SHOUTS BACK.

THE NEXT FEW MILES ARE AN IMPROMPTU CRITICAL MASS RIDE. THE FOUR OF US FORM A SLOW MOVING BOTTLENECK THAT BRINGS ROUTE 51 — FEARSOME, NOTORIOUS ROUTE 51 — TO ITS KNEES. A LONG LINE OF CARS BEGINS TO PILE UP BEHIND US. AT SOME POINT, WE PASS SOME CONSTRUCTION WORKERS. THEY LOOK AT US. THEY LOOK AT THE TRAFFIC JAMMED UP BEHIND US. THE SITUATION IS GETTING A LITTLE OUT OF HAND, SO WHEN WE ARRIVE AT AN EMERGENCY PULL-OFF, WE DUCK IN AND LET THE TRAFFIC PASS. WHAT FOLLOWS IS AN AGONIZINGLY LONG LINE OF ROAD RAGING DRIVERS, EACH OF WHOM

TAKES THE OPPORTUNITY TO HONK, OR GIVE US THE FINGER, OR SHOUT SOMETHING. THE WHOLE THING IS LIKE RUNNING THE GAUNTLET IN REVERSE: THE GAUNTLET MOVES AND WE STAY PUT.

SOMEHOW WE ESCAPE THE CONSTRUCTION ZONE ALIVE, AND SPEND THE NEXT FEW HOURS FOLLOWING "PENN BIKE ROUTE A," A CRUEL JOKE OF A BIKE ROUTE MAPPED OUT BY A BIKE-HATING LUNATIC. THE ROADS ARE BUSY AND FAST, PUNCTUATED BY LITTLE TOWNS – NEW BRIGHTON, ROCHESTER – WHOSE CHARMS ARE OBSCURED BY THE THOUGHT THAT, ANY SECOND NOW, I'M GOING TO GET CRUSHED BY A SEMI.

PAST BEAVER FALLS, WE DETOUR OFF THE STATE BIKE ROUTE AND TAKE A

SHORTCUT I DEVISED WITH THE HELP OF GOOGLE MAPS. I BRAG THAT MY ROUTE WILL SHAVE 5 MILES OFF THE DAY'S RIDE. WHAT I DIDN'T REALIZE IS THAT THE SHORTCUT TAKES US OVER THE TOP OF A MOUNTAIN. IN NO TIME, WE'VE CLICKED DOWN TO OUR LOWEST GEARS, AND WHEN WE'VE RUN OUT OF GEARS TO CLICK DOWN TO, WE GET OFF OUR BIKES AND PUSH. WE PUSH OUR BIKES FOR A VERY LONG TIME. NO ONE SAYS A WORD.

THEN, HALF DEAD, WE CROSS INTO OHIO. THE SUN IS SETTING BY THE TIME WE GET TO PETERSBURG. RENATO AND I BROWSE THROUGH THE SNACK AISLE AT THE GAS STATION WHILE LJR AND TED WANDER OVER TO SMITTY'S TAVERN.

"YOUR FRIENDS SHOULD BE CAREFUL," THE GIRL AT THE REGISTER TELLS US, "THAT PLACE HAS A BAD CROWD."

LJR AND TED RETURN WITH A MAP TO JEFF'S HOUSE.

"WHO THE HELL IS JEFF?" I ASK.

"HE WAS AT SMITTY'S" LJR SAYS.

"HE SAYS WE CAN CAMP IN HIS BACK YARD," TED SAYS.

"HE LOOKS LIKE JOHNNY FEVER FROM WKRP IN CINCINNATI," LJR SAYS.

I DON'T LIKE THIS PLAN, BUT I'M OVERRULED. SO WE FOLLOW THE DIRECTIONS TO JEFF'S HOUSE, WHERE WE FIND JEFF WAITING FOR US. HE'S A GUY IN HIS 50'S WITH BUSHY BROWN HAIR AND A BUSHY BROWN MUSTACHE. THE HOUSE IS ON A CUL-DE

SAC IN A BRAND NEW DEVELOPMENT THAT WAS RECENTLY CARVED OUT OF A CORN FIELD. JEFF TAKES US AROUND BACK WHERE THERE'S A VAST GRASSY YARD THAT MERGES WITH THE GRASSY YARDS OF ALL THE OTHER HOUSES ON ALL THE OTHER CUL-DE-SACS. JEFF POINTS TO THE HOUSE NEXT DOOR. "THAT PLACE BELONGS TO THE PILOT." THEN HE POINTS TO A LONG STRIP OF GRASS CUT LOW LIKE A PUTTING GREEN. "THAT'S HIS AIRSTRIP. WHATEVER THE PILOT WANTS, HE BUYS." WHILE WE PITCH OUR TENTS, TED HELPS JEFF BUILD A CAMPFIRE NEXT TO THE VEGETABLE GARDEN. ALL AROUND US, A WILDERNESS OF HOT TUBS AND TRAMPOLINES. BIG SCREEN TV'S FLICKER IN THE DISTANCE LIKE FIRE-FLIES.

ONCE THE FIRE'S GOING, WE SIT AROUND IT AND JEFF TELLS US HE DIGS DITCHES FOR A LIVING. FOR FIBER OPTIC LINES, IT TURNS OUT. THE KIND OF DITCH DIGGING THAT PAYS PRETTY WELL. JEFF TELLS US HE GREW UP IN OHIO. HIS FAMILY HAD A FARM WITH A BRICK-MAKING OPERATION ON IT. THERE WERE CLAY MINES AND KILNS ALL OVER THIS PART OF THE STATE. BUT THEN THE BRICK INDUSTRY CRASHED, ALONG WITH EVERY OTHER INDUSTRY AROUND HERE. THE COAL MINES CLOSED AND SO DID THE STEEL MILLS AND THE CAR FACTORIES.

THEN JEFF'S WIFE GETS HOME. BACK AT SMITTY'S, JEFF SAID HE'D CALL HIS WIFE TO MAKE SURE IT WAS OK FOR US TO VISIT. BUT JEFF NEVER MADE THE CALL. MAYBE IT'S THE CAMPFIRE NEXT TO HER

VEGETABLE GARDEN, OR MAYBE IT'S FINDING RENATO WASHING HIS BIKE SHORTS IN THE KITCHEN SINK, BUT JEFF'S WIFE ISN'T PLEASED TO SEE US. "JEFFREY, GET THE FUCK IN HERE!" SHE YELLS FROM THE BACK PORCH. JEFF SIGHS AND GOES INSIDE THE HOUSE. WE HEAR SOME YELLING ABOUT HOW JEFF IS A DRUNKEN IDIOT. THEN THE PORCH LIGHT GOES OUT AND JEFF COMES BACK TO THE CAMPFIRE. THIS GOES ON FOR A WHILE: THE PORCH LIGHT SNAPS ON; JEFF'S WIFE YELLS SOMETHING LIKE "JEFFREY, I'M CALLING THE POLICE!"; THEN JEFF SHUFFLES INSIDE AND TURNS OFF THE PORCH LIGHT. AROUND 1 AM, JEFF SAYS GOODNIGHT. AT SOME POINT IN THE MIDDLE OF THE NIGHT, I SNEAK OUT OF MY TENT AS QUIETLY AS I CAN,

UNZIPPING MY TENT FLAP ONE ZIPPER TOOTH AT A TIME. THEN I TIP-TOE BEHIND AN ORNAMENTAL SHRUB AND TAKE A PEE, PRAYING THAT THE PORCH LIGHT DOESN'T SNAP ON.

IN THE MORNING, WE PACK UP OUR TENTS AND WAIT AROUND A WHILE TO SAY GOODBYE TO JEFF, BUT JEFF NEVER COMES OUT. SO WE ROLL DOWN THE DRIVEWAY AND INTO THE CUL-DE-SAC AND BACK ONTO THE ROAD.

08/18/06

EASTERN OHIO IS AN ASPHALT ROLLER COASTER. EVERY 30MPH DOWNHILL THRILL RIDE HAS TO BE PAID FOR IN FULL BY AN AGONIZING UPHILL GRIND. IT'S PRETTY, THIS STATE OF ROLLING CORNFIELDS AND CENTURY-OLD BARNS. BUT ALL I SEE ARE THE HILLS, LIKE

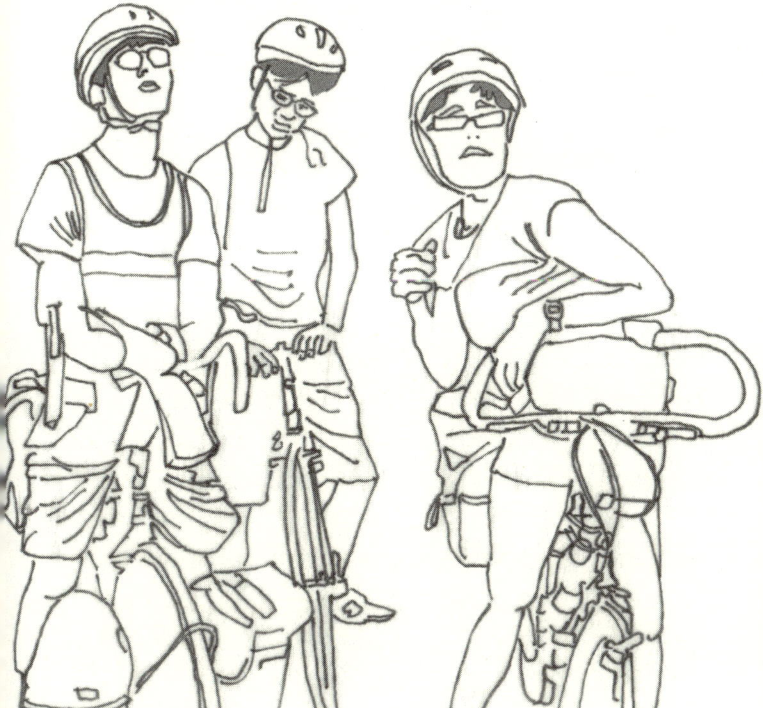

A LONG LINE OF SUMO WRESTLERS, EACH ONE GRABBING ME AROUND THE WAIST AND TOSSING ME TO THE GROUND.

WE RIDE A ROUTE CALLED THE CARDINAL TRAIL, MAPPED OUT BY A GROUP OF CYCLISTS FROM COLUMBUS CALLED OUTDOOR PURSUITS. THE ROUTE AVOIDS BUSY ROADS WITH SOMETHING CLOSE TO A RELIGIOUS FERVOR. EVERY TIME I GLIMPSE A BIG, TRUCK-INFESTED HIGHWAY OFF IN THE DISTANCE, I SILENTLY THANK THESE ANONYMOUS OUTDOOR PURSUIT-ISTS FOR THEIR OUTSTANDING WORK. THE ONLY PROBLEM WITH THE ROUTE IS THAT IT'S REALLY COMPLICATED. IMAGINE GIVING SOMEONE WHO LIVES ON THE OTHER SIDE OF YOUR STATE DIRECTIONS TO YOUR HOUSE, BUT THEY HAVE TO STICK TO SIDE STREETS.

GO LEFT 0.3 MILES, THEN RIGHT 0.1 MILES, THEN VEER LEFT IN 100 YARDS — IT'S LIKE THAT. WE HAVE TO STOP AGAIN AND AGAIN TO CHECK THE MAPS AND WE KEEP GETTING LOST. IT GETS DARK BEFORE WE FIND A PLACE TO STAY FOR THE NIGHT, SO WE DETOUR INTO ALLIANCE, HOPING TO FIND A MOTEL ROOM. WE RIDE THE LAST COUPLE MILES ON A PITCH BLACK COUNTRY HIGHWAY WITH NO SHOULDER AND LOTS OF TRAFFIC. ROAD KILL KEEPS FLARING UP IN THE HEADLIGHTS OF CARS THAT COME UP FAST BEHIND US. IT'S LIKE AN OLD HORROR MOVIE, WHERE THE ROAD TO DRACULA'S CASTLE IS LITTERED WITH CORPSES.

08/19/06

OUTSIDE ALLIANCE, THE TROUBLE BEGINS. TED'S KNEES SWELL, LJR'S SEAT BREAKS, THE SKY CLOUDS UP, AND THE ROAD GETS CHOKED WITH CARS HEADING TO A NASCAR RACE. AS WE SLOG ON TOWARD NORTH CANTON, THE FIELDS BEGIN TO SPROUT MORE TRACT HOMES THAN CORN COBS. JUST AS THE RAIN STARTS, TED SPOTS A RESTAURANT ALONG THE HIGHWAY. "THE 365TH FIGHTER GROUP," IT'S CALLED. WE LOCK OUR BIKES TO THE WORLD WAR TWO ARTILLERY GUN THAT SITS OUT FRONT. INSIDE, THE DECORATING LOOKS LIKE A COLLABORATION BETWEEN G.I. JOE AND SOMEBODY'S FRENCH GRANDMOTHER. THERE ARE SANDBAGS AND BARBED WIRE AND VASES FILLED WITH ARTIFICIAL FLOWERS THAT SIT ON ANTIQUE TABLES. IN THE MEN'S

ROOM, A RECORDING OF A WINSTON CHURCHILL SPEECH PLAYS IN AN ENDLESS LOOP: "WE SHALL FIGHT IN THE FIELDS AND IN THE STREETS, WE SHALL FIGHT IN THE HILLS, WE SHALL NEVER SURRENDER." WE ORDER LUNCH THEN SIT AROUND FOR ANOTHER HOUR, WAITING OUT THE RAIN WITH, WE HOPE, THE SAME CALM COMPOSURE OF SOME G.I.'S WAITING OUT A GERMAN BOMBARDMENT.

THAT NIGHT, WE FIND A CAMPGROUND CALLED CAMELOT. IT'S RUN BY AN OLD GUY NAMED DAN AND HIS DOG, CANDY. WE'RE THE ONLY PEOPLE THERE. WE ASK DAN IF THERE'S ANY PLACE TO GET FOOD, AND HE TELLS US THE NEAREST CONVENIENCE

STORE IS FIVE MILES AWAY. SO WE SCROUNGE THROUGH OUR PANNIERS AND COME UP WITH DINNER: PEANUT BUTTER AND RAMEN NOODLE SANDWICHES ON WHEAT BREAD. AT FIRST, WE THINK THEY'RE DELICIOUS. IN FACT, WE THINK WE MAY HAVE MADE A SIGNIFICANT CONTRIBUTION TO CAMPGROUND CUISINE. BUT AFTER A FEW MORE BITES, WE COME TO OUR SENSES.

AFTER DINNER, WE HANG OUT IN THE GAME ROOM, A CINDERBLOCK HALL WITH A LOPSIDED POOL TABLE IN THE MIDDLE. DAN THE OWNER DROPS BY AND TELLS US ABOUT HIS WORLD TRAVELS AS A FREELANCE BRICK MASON. HE'S BEEN EVERYWHERE. IN EGYPT, HE MET A FOXY RUSSIAN ENGINEER WHO WAS WORKING ON THE ASWAN HIGH DAM. IN HOLLYWOOD, HE DID BRICK WORK FOR THE STARS.

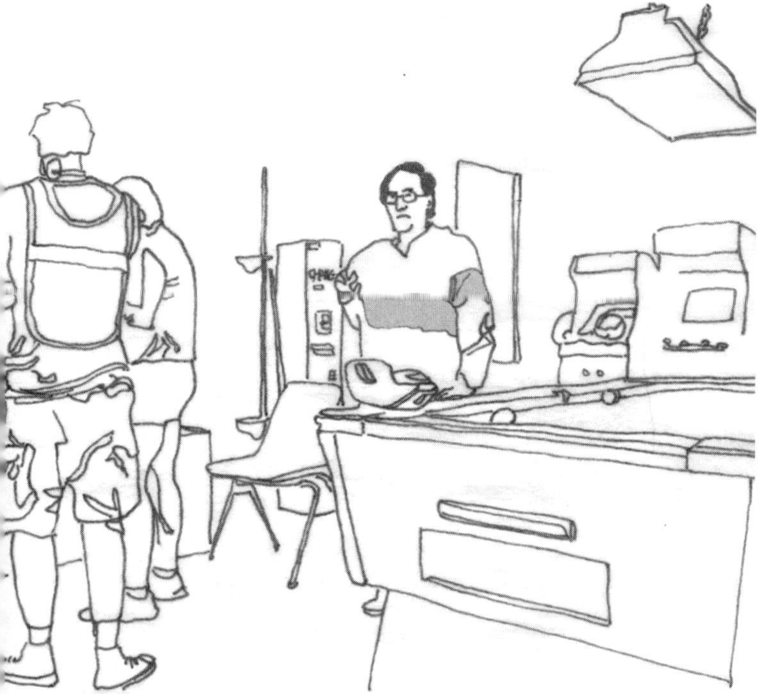

HE DISCOVERED THAT MOST CELEB-
RITIES LIVE SAD, DRUNKEN LIVES.
"EXCEPT BURT LANCASTER,"
DAN TELLS US. "BURT LANCASTER
WAS A REAL DOWN-TO-EARTH GUY."

LATE THAT NIGHT, THE RACCOONS
STRIKE. LOTS OF THEM. THOUSANDS,
MAYBE MORE. TED TRIES TO
SCARE THEM OFF BY PLAYING
A SAMPLING OF RING TONES ON
HIS CELL PHONE, BUT IT DOESN'T
WORK. IT'D TAKE SILVER BULLETS
OR WOODEN STAKES THROUGH THE
HEART TO STOP THESE RACCOONS.
WHEN WE FINALLY SCRAMBLE OUT OF OUR
TENTS AND CHASE THEM AWAY, WE
DISCOVER THAT THEY'VE EATEN A
WHOLE BAG OF FIG NEWTONS AND
HAVE EVEN MANAGED TO RAID TED'S
PANNIER AND OPEN HIS BOTTLE OF

HERBAL VITAMINS. TED IS PRETTY SHAKEN UP. "THAT BOTTLE HAD A CHILDPROOF CAP," HE SAYS, INCREDULOUS.

08/20/06

I HAD TO CANCEL THE SCREENING IN FT. WAYNE, INDIANA. WE'RE ALREADY TWO DAYS BEHIND SCHEDULE, AND THERE'S NO CHANCE WE'D GET THERE IN TIME. I'M BEGINNING TO WONDER WHETHER I'LL HAVE TO CANCEL THE WHOLE DAMN MOVIE TOUR.

WE SPEND THE DAY RIDING UP AND DOWN A LANDSCAPE OUR MAP DESCRIBES AS "SCENIC ROLLING FARMLAND." WE STOP FOR DINNER AT A CONVENIENCE STORE / VIDEO RENTAL SHOP/ LIQUOR STORE / PIZZERIA AT THE CORNER OF RT. 301

AND RT. 302. IF RURAL OHIO HAS ONE PRIME INTERSECTION, THIS IS PROBABLY IT. A NEVER-ENDING PARADE OF HARLEYS, FARM TRACTORS, PICKUP TRUCKS, ATV'S, AMISH BUGGIES, AND BITCHIN' CAMAROS ROLL UP TO THE FOUR-WAY STOP AND PAUSE JUST LONG ENOUGH TO GIVE US A DIRTY LOOK. EXCEPT FOR THE AMISH KIDS. THEY SMILE AND WAVE, AND WE WAVE BACK. MAYBE THE AMISH KIDS RECOGNIZE US AS KINDRED SPIRITS: NO MOTORS, SLOW MOVING, AND NOT EXACTLY POPULAR WITH THE DRIVERS.

WE FIND A GOOD CAMPGROUND JUST DOWN THE ROAD. IT'S A TIDY PLACE RUN BY AN OLD HIPPY LADY WITH A BIG BOOMING VOICE. "WELCOME, BIKERS!" SHE BOOMS.

"YOU GET THE BIKE RIDER DISCOUNT!"
"YOU HAVE A BIKE DISCOUNT?" LJR ASKS.

"NO!" SHE BOOMS, "BUT I LIKE YOU!"

THERE IS A STACK OF INDIVIDUAL-SIZED PEACH PIES SITTING NEXT TO THE CASH REGISTER. WE EACH BUY ONE. BACK AT THE CAMPSITE, TED LIGHTS A FIRE — TED IS GETTING GOOD AT LIGHTING CAMP FIRES — AND WE SIT IN THE SOFT GRASS AND EAT OUR LITTLE PIES.

08/21/06

THIS MORNING IS CUT OUT OF GLASS. LIKE THE HOLE A DIAMOND THIEF CUTS IN THE PLATE GLASS WINDOW OF A JEWELRY STORE. PERFECT AND PRECISE. WE RIDE

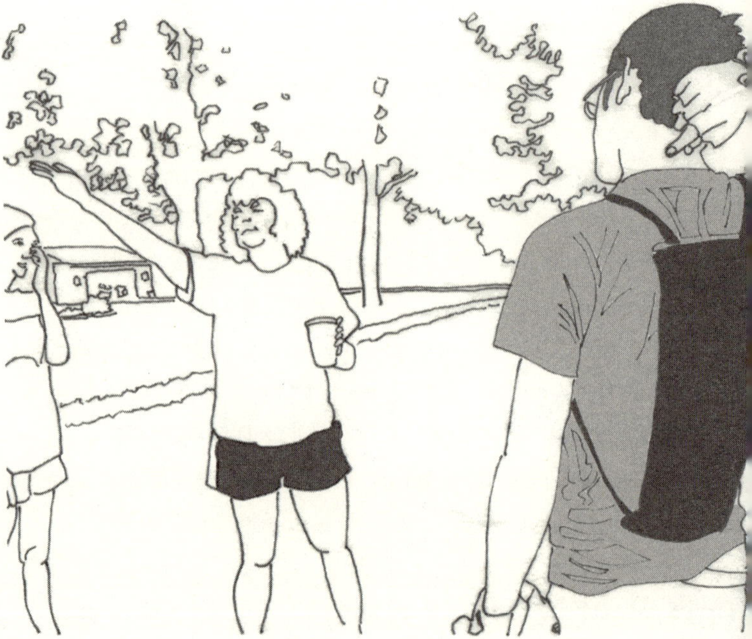

PAST OLD FARMHOUSES WEIGHTED DOWN WITH VICTORIAN WOODWORK. WINDOWS WITH HEAVY WOODEN LIDS, AND ROOFS PERCHED ON INTRICATELY CARVED CORNICES. SURPRISING DECORATIVE FLOURISHES ON HOUSES THAT IN EVERY OTHER WAY ARE STRIPPED DOWN AND SEVERE. MAYBE THIS IS WHERE 19TH CENTURY OHIO FARMERS HINTED AT THE CRAZY, UNCONTROLLED PASSIONS BURIED UP INSIDE THEM – IN THESE LITTLE ARCHITECTURAL DETAILS. THE PARTS OF OHIO THAT AREN'T PLANTED IN CORN ARE PLANTED IN SOYBEANS, AND THE REST IS PLANTED IN GRASS; VAST ROLLING LAWNS THAT OLD MEN ON SIT-DOWN MOWERS SPEND THEIR RETIREMENT YEARS CUTTING IN STRAIGHT LINES.

WE RIDE THROUGH JEROMESVILLE AND HAYESVILLE. OHIO ROLLS, SOMETIMES SLOW AND SMOOTH, AND SOMETIMES IT LUNGES AND WE FREE FALL DOWN ONE SIDE OF A HILL AND CRAWL UP THE OTHER. OUTSIDE MANSFIELD, THE TRAFFIC PICKS UP. MANSFIELD IS AN OLD INDUSTRIAL TOWN, THE KIND OF PLACE YOU'D EXPECT TO FIND UP NEAR CLEVELAN. OR TOLEDO, BUT THAT SEEMS OUT OF PLACE DOWN HERE IN FARM COUNTRY. IT'S FAMOUS AS THE HOME OF THE HIGHWAY SAFETY FOUNDATION, WHICH PRODUCED A SERIES OF GRUESOME DRIVER'S ED SCARE FILMS LIKE "MECHANIZED DEATH" AND "HIGHWAYS OF AGONY." THE FILMS OFTEN USED ACCIDENT FOOTAGE

FROM AROUND MANSFIELD. AS WE RIDE INTO TOWN, WE COME UP WITH TITLES FOR BIKE-RELATED SCARE FILMS: "PEDALS OF PAIN," "TOE CLIPS OF TERROR," ETC.

AFTER SO MANY MILES OF RIDING ON A BAD SEAT WITHOUT BIKE SHORTS, TED'S BUTT IS IN CRITICAL CONDITION. WE GO LOOKING FOR A NEW BIKE SEAT. WE FIND A SHOP CALLED 'BEST BIKE.' IT'S RUN BY A MIDDLE-AGED STORM CHASER AND HIS SWEET OLD MOM. THE SON SHOWS US SNAPSHOTS FROM THE ANNUAL CROSS-OHIO BIKE RIDE. IT'S A HUGE THING: 3000 CYCLISTS, INCLUDING A GUY NAMED CHRIS CAKE, WHO IS FAMOUS FOR THE

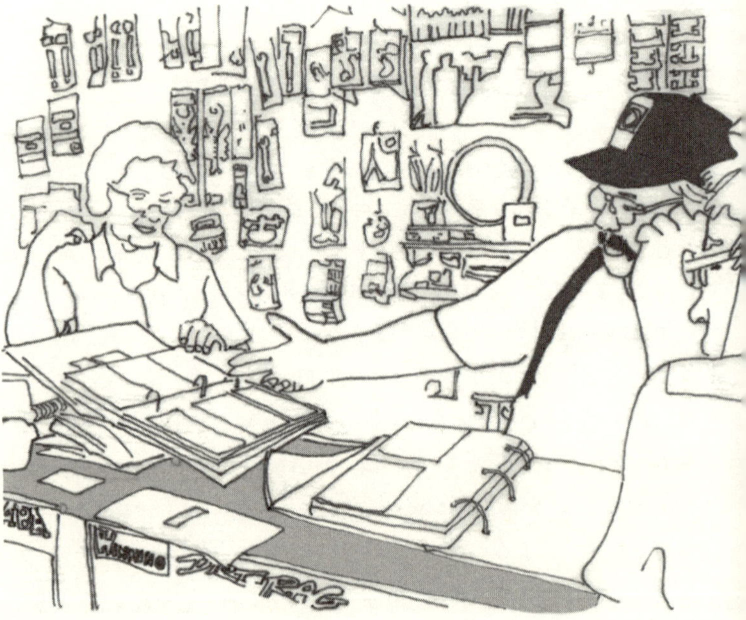

HEIGHT OF HIS PANCAKE FLIPS, AS WELL AS HIS ACCURACY WHEN TOSSING PANCAKES ONTO PLATES.

THE BIKE SHOP GUY RECOMMENDS A MEXICAN RESTAURANT WHERE THE MARGARITAS ARE STIFF. WE SIT AROUND TILL THE WAITERS START STACKING THE CHAIRS ON THE TABLES. THEN WE STUMBLE OUTSIDE AND RIDE ALL WOBBLY AND WHOOPING IT UP THROUGH THE EMPTY STREETS. FORGETTING FOR A WHILE THAT WE'RE IN THE TOWN WHERE "CARRIER OR KILLER" WAS PRODUCED. HAPPY JUST TO RIDE THROUGH A WARM AUGUST NIGHT, AND TO BE 500 MILES FROM D.C. AND A MILLION MILES FROM ANYWHERE ELSE.

08/22/06

LJR IS GONE. WE WAKE UP THIS MORNING WITH CHEAP TEQUILA HEADACHES, AND AS WE'RE CHECKING OUT OF THE MOTEL, SHE TELLS US SHE'S CATCHING A BUS BACK TO CHICAGO. ONE MINUTE SHE'S THERE, AND THE NEXT MINUTE, WE'RE STANDING IN FRONT OF A BOB EVANS, WAVING GOODBYE.

THE STORM CHASER AT BEST BIKE IS RIGHT: JUST WEST OF MANSFIELD, THE TERRAIN STARTS TO FLATTEN OUT. AFTER THE HARD GRIND OF EASTERN OHIO, IT'S LIKE OUR BIKES HAVE ADDED JET ENGINES. WE ZIP ALONG. BUCYRUS. NEVADA (THE FIRST 'A' IS LONG). SANDUSKY. WE FINALLY PULL INTO A CONVENIENCE STORE AND ASK THE

GUY AT THE REGISTER WHERE WE CAN STOP FOR THE NIGHT. WE POINT TO SOME TOWNS ON OUR MAP. CAREY, OR MAYBE VANLUE. THE GUY LAUGHS. "THOSE ARE ONE-BLINK TOWNS, EVEN IF YOU'RE PASSING THROUGH AT BIKE SPEED."

HE TELLS US HE THINKS THERE'S A CAMPGROUND OUTSIDE A LITTLE TOWN CALLED LOVELL, SO THAT'S WHERE WE RIDE. THE ROADS ARE QUIET LANES THAT CUT THROUGH CORNFIELDS. QUIET AND CAREFREE TILL THE DOGS ATTACK. FARM DOGS CHARGE FROM THE LEFT, AND THEY CHARGE FROM THE RIGHT, AND THEY COME RUNNING UP THE ROAD BEHIND US, BLOCKING OUR RETREAT.

"THEY'RE TRIANGULATING!" RENATO YELLS. "RUN FOR IT!"

WE PEDAL AS HARD AS WE CAN, DOGS IN HOT PURSUIT. BUT THEY'RE FARM DOGS, AND ONCE WE'VE LEFT THEIR TURF, THEY BREAK OFF THE CHASE AND PRANCE BACK HOME, FEELING ALL BAD ASS.

THE TEE PEE CAMPGROUND IS REALLY AN RV PARK WHERE EVERYONE IS A FULL-TIME RESIDENT. WE FIND THE OFFICE, BUT IT'S CLOSED. WHILE WE'RE STANDING THERE, A COUPLE OLD GUYS ROAR UP IN THEIR TRICKED-OUT GOLF CART. IT'S GOT SPANGLES HANGING FROM THE ROOF AND AIRBRUSHED FLAMES SHOOTING OUT BEHIND THE TIRES. IT'S EVEN GOT CHROME SPINNER HUBCAPS.

"WHOA. A GANGSTA GOLF CART," TED WHISPERS.

"YOU LOOKIN' FOR A CAMP SITE?" THE DRIVER ASKS.

"YES," WE TELL HIM.

"FOLLOW ME, BOYS!" HE CALLS, SHOOTING GRAVEL AS HE FLOORS IT.

WE PITCH OUR TENTS NEAR SOME RAILROAD TRACKS. IT'S A BUSY LINE. EVERY HOUR OR SO, A FREIGHT TRAIN RUMBLES BY. I LIE AWAKE FOR A LONG TIME, LISTENING TO THE LONELY SOUND OF TRAIN WHISTLES, AND THE QUIET THAT COMES AFTER. THINKING ABOUT ALL THE EMPTY SPACE I'VE RIDDEN THROUGH. IT'S EASY TO FORGET WHEN YOU'RE LIVING IN A CITY THAT THIS COUNTRY IS MOSTLY EMPTY LIKE THAT. ONE-BLINK TOWNS AND THE TWO LANE ROADS IN BETWEEN.

08/23/06

BREAKFAST IS PEACH PIE FILLING THAT THE LADY AT THE DINER SCOOPS INTO PLASTIC BOWLS.

"I PICKED THE PEACHES OFF THE TREE IN MY BACKYARD," SHE TELLS US. AFTER WE EAT, RENATO SLIPS ON HIS COLLEGE CYCLING TEAM JERSEY.

"TODAY WE'LL DO A METRIC CENTURY," HE ANNOUNCES.

A METRIC CENTURY IS WHEN YOU RIDE 100 KM. CYCLISTS ARE ALWAYS TALKING ABOUT CENTURY RIDES. A CYCLIST WHO CAN RIDE 100 MILES IN A DAY IS HARDCORE. A CYCLIST WHO CAN RIDE 100 KM IN A DAY IS METRICALLY HARDCORE, WHICH IS ABOUT 2/3 AS HARDCORE. WE RIDE

PAST FARM FIELDS, TRAILER HOMES, SOYBEANS, AND DOGS. ALWAYS DOGS, WHO GO CRAZY WITH HATE AT THE SIGHT OF BIKE RIDERS. WORSE THAN JOCK BOYS, THOSE DOGS. THE JOCKS DON'T USUALLY CHASE YOU, BUT THE DOGS ALWAYS DO.

WE RIDE. KILOMETER AFTER KILO-METER. SOUTH OF OTTAWA, AND WELL SHORT OF A CENTURY, WE START TO FALL APART.

"MY ARMS FEEL FUNNY," TED SAYS IN A FUNNY WAY.

WE FIND A MEXICAN JOINT IN TOWN CALLED LOS MARIACHIS AND GOBBLE UP A FEW BASKETS OF CHIPS AND SALSA. THEN WE GET A ROOM IN THE ONLY MOTEL IN PUTNAM COUNTY, OHIO. AT MIDNIGHT, WE ALL WAKE UP WITH BAD GAS PAINS, WHICH WE DUB 'THE CURSE OF

LOS MARIACHIS.'

08/24/06

WE GET TO GROVER HILL BY 3PM AND PULL UP IN FRONT OF A PIZZA PLACE CALLED THE DEPOT. IT'S CLOSED, LIKE EVERYTHING ELSE IN TOWN. AS WE START TO WALK AWAY, THE GUY WHO RUNS THE PLACE UNLOCKS THE DOOR AND INVITES US IN. HE'S A COMPACT, MIDDLE-AGED GUY WITH A MUSTACHE AND A T-SHIRT WITH THE WORDS "STOCK CAR RACING" OVER A PICTURE OF A RED-WHITE-AND-BLUE RACE CAR. WE ASK FOR A VEGAN PIZZA. HE SHRUGS. "IT'S YOUR PIZZA." THE GUY TELLS US THAT GROVER HILL USED TO HAVE FOUR RESTAURANTS, BUT NOW IT'S JUST HIM. WE ASK HIM WHAT HAPPENED.

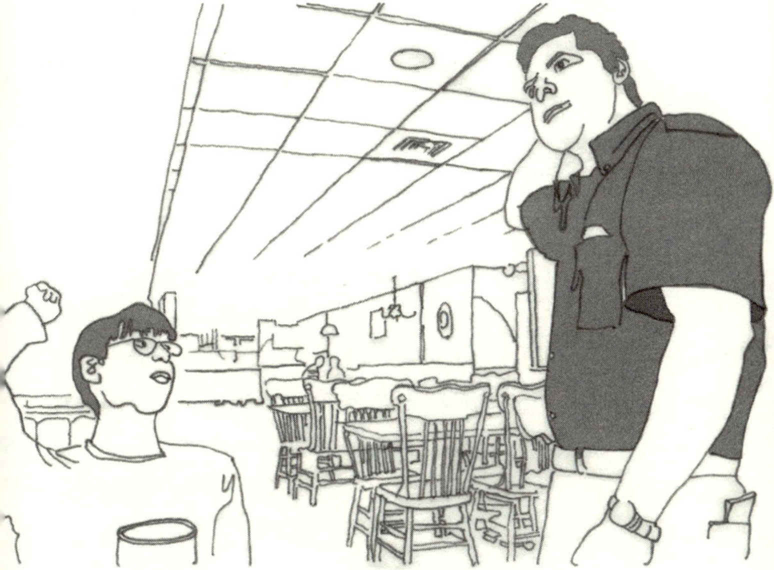

"IT'S THE PEOPLE WHO RUN THIS TOWN IS WHY IT'S GONE TO POT."

HE POINTS TO THE BANK ACROSS THE STREET. MOST OF THE BUILDINGS WE PASSED ON THE WAY INTO TOWN WERE RUNDOWN, BUT THE BANK IS PRETTY NICE. IT HAS A FANCY L.E.D. SIGN OUT FRONT THAT FLASHES THE TIME AND TEMP. INSTEAD OF A BANK NAME, THOUGH, THERE'S A BANNER HANGING ON THE BUILDING THAT SAYS "BUY A BANK!" THE PIZZA GUY TELLS US THE BANK PRESIDENT WAS A LOCAL, AND MOST EVERYBODY IN TOWN KEPT THEIR MONEY THERE. THEN, A COUPLE YEARS AGO, THE PRESIDENT WAS BUSTE FOR STEALING MONEY FROM THE BANK. LOTS OF MONEY, WHICH HE INVESTED IN GAMBLING BOATS IN SOUTH

CAROLINA. GROVER HILL NEVER REALLY RECOVERED FROM THIS.

WHEN OUR PIZZA'S READY, THE GUY BRINGS IT OVER AND SITS DOWN WITH US. HE TELLS US HE USED TO BE A TRUCK DRIVER, BUT HE WASN'T CUT OUT FOR IT. "I GOT A BREAKING POINT," HE EXPLAINS. "WHEN I'M ABOUT TO SNAP, YOU BETTER PAY ATTENTION." HE TELLS US ABOUT ONE GUY WHO DIDN'T PAY ATTENTION. HE GRABBED THE GUY BY THE EARS AND BEAT HIS HEAD AGAINST A WOODEN BENCH. "I HOPE ONE OF THOSE SPLINTERS GOES INTO YOUR BRAIN," HE SCREAMED AT THE GUY. WE TAKE THIS IN AS WE WORK OUR WAY THROUGH OUR CHEESE-FREE, ALL-VEGGIE PIZZA. WHEN WE FINISH,

WE PAY THE BILL AND LEAVE A TIP. A REALLY BIG TIP.

THE INDIANA STATE LINE IS ABOUT 20 MILES DOWN THE ROAD, AND RENATO SETS A BLISTERING PACE. ONLY ONE STATE LIES BETWEEN HIM AND CHICAGO, AND HE'S STARTING TO FEEL THE TUG OF IT; THE GRAVITATIONAL PULL OF HIS FINAL DESTINATION. AT STATE LINE ROAD, WE TAKE A BREATHER. A LADY ACROSS THE STREET IS WATERING HER LAWN.

"WOULD YOU LIKE SOME WATER?" SHE CALLS TO US FROM INDIANA.

"SURE!" WE CALL BACK FROM OHIO.

08/25/06

RENATO IS UP AT THE CRACK OF DAWN. HE WANTS TO DO A CENTURY RIDE

Bank fraud case stuns town

By **John Seewer**
The Associated Press

OAKWOOD, Ohio — Just about every morning, Mark Miller would walk through the back door of the town's bar and grill and say hello to the regulars.

Talk over coffee usually centered around the weather and sports at the high school, where Mr. Miller was a fixture on the board. His brother was the school's principal, and family members helped coach its teams.

Then, the bank executive vice president would walk next door to work at the Oakwood Deposit Bank — where federal prosecutors say he embezzled $40 million for years from friends and neighbors in the farming town of 700 people.

The Federal Deposit Insurance Corp. seized and closed the bank's two branches, in Oakwood and nearby Grover Hill, on Feb. 1. The bank has reopened under the management of The State Bank and Trust Co.

The collapse of this Paulding County town's only bank, which stood since 1905 and weathered droughts and the Depression, has stunned and saddened folks in northwest Ohio's farm belt. It has left a school district and a community struggling to recover.

Much of the money went to casino boats in the South, prosecutors said. Mr. Miller also bought a horse farm and time shares — all while living with his wife and three children in a modest single-story brick home.

The Wayne Trace school district and the county-owned hospital each lost nearly $1 million. And the village of Oakwood lost all of its $350,000 savings, forcing it to lay off five workers and cut everything but emergency repairs.

"We're in trouble. Big trouble," said Bud Henke, Oakwood' Village Council president. "All the town's money was in there."

Janet Ross said she and her husband lost $40,000 in stocks, which they planned to pass on to their children.

"The saddest thing is that he destroyed a business that's been here through some real hard times," said Ms. Ross, who runs a gas station in Grover Hill.

Generations of farmers have brought their crops to the grain elevators that tower above the towns and then deposited their checks at the bank.

TODAY, A REAL ONE, AND ANOTHER ONE TOMORROW. A MAD DASH TO CHICAGO FOR REASONS HE DOESN'T DISCLOSE, BUT THAT I SUSPECT HAVE SOMETHING TO DO WITH ROMANCE. THAT, OR HE'S JUST SICK OF THE RIDE. TED AND I SAY GOODBYE, THEN SLEEP A FEW MORE HOURS. THIS WILL START TO BECOME A ROUTINE WITH TED AND ME. WITHOUT RENATO AROUND, WE GET SLOWER AND SLOPPIER.

BREAKFAST IS AT AN OLD COFFEE SHOP CALLED HALLS. THE PLACE IS HIDDEN BEHIND THE THICKET OF FAST FOOD JOINTS THAT LINE THE MAIN DRAG OF NEW HAVEN, INDIANA. THIS MORNING, I DON'T FEEL LIKE MAKING APOLOGIES FOR THE FAST FOOD JOINTS. I HATE THEM. AND

WHILE GETTING PECAN WAFFLES AT HALLS ISN'T A CURE, EXACTLY, IT HELPS TAKE THE EDGE OFF.

08/26/06

WHEN WE WAKE UP, IT'S POURING. THE TV SAYS THERE'S RAIN CLEAR ACROSS INDIANA. THE SENSIBLE THING TO DO IS HUNKER DOWN IN THE MOTEL, BUT I'M DUE IN LAFAYETTE FOR A SCREENING ON THE DAY AFTER TOMORROW.

"IS THERE A BUS FROM HERE TO LAFAYETTE?" I ASK THE GUY AT THE FRONT DESK. HE SHAKES HIS HEAD.

"THERE'S A BUS TO FT. WAYNE, THAT'S ALL," HE TELLS ME.

IT TURNS OUT IT'S NOT SO EASY TO GET FROM HUNTINGTON, INDIANA — THAT'S WHERE WE'RE STAYING — TO LAFAYETTE. FIRST,

YOU TAKE A BUS TO FT. WAYNE. FROM THERE, YOU CATCH ANOTHER BUS TO INDIANAPOLIS. THEN, AFTER A TWELVE HOUR LAYOVER, YOU GET ON THE BUS TO LAFAYETTE. THE GUY AT THE FRONT DESK FEELS SORRY FOR US, SO HE CALLS THE HEAD HOUSEKEEPER, A NO-NONSENSE LADY WITH BIG BICEPS AND TWO EX-HUSBANDS, NEITHER OF WHOM IS INTERESTED IN GIVING US A LIFT. FINALLY, SHE CALLS HER BROTHER, AND HE AGREES TO HELP US OUT. AN HOUR LATER, HE SHOWS UP AT THE MOTEL IN A MINIVAN FULL OF LITTLE KIDS. HIS NAME IS RAY. HE'S A BIG GUY WITH A SCRAGGLY BEARD AND A BASEBALL HAT WITH AN AMERICAN FLAG ON THE FRONT. TED AND I OFFER HIM SOME CASH AND A TANK OF GAS IF HE'LL TAKE US TO LAFAYETTE. HE PUFFS ON HIS CIGARETTE FOR A MINUTE, MULLING IT OVER.

"OKAY," HE SAYS, "BUT IT'LL HAVE

TO BE LATER." LATER, IT TURNS OUT, IS 3 HOURS LATER. TED AND I KILL A FEW HOURS AT THE PUBLIC LIBRARY. WHEN IT'S TIME TO MEET RAY, WE STAND OUT FRONT WITH OUR BIKES. A FRIENDLY LADY NOTICES US, AND SHE ASKS US ABOUT OUR BIKE TRIP. WHEN WE MENTION WE'RE CATCHING A RIDE WITH A STRANGER, SHE INSISTS ON WAITING WITH US. I HADN'T BEEN ALL THAT NERVOUS ABOUT RIDING WITH RAY, BUT THANKS TO THIS LADY, NOW I'M NERVOUS. WHEN HE FINALLY PULLS UP IN HIS BEAT-UP MINIVAN, I CAN TELL BY HER EXPRESSION THAT THIS LADY THINKS WE'RE DEAD. RAY HELPS US CRAM OUR BIKES INTO THE BACK OF HIS MINIVAN, PILING THEM ON TOP OF THE BABY STROLLERS AND AUTO PARTS AND PILES OF CLOTHES THAT HIS CAR IS FULL OF. MEANWHILE, THE FRIENDLY LADY ASKS RAY

WHAT HIS NAME IS AND WHERE HE'S FROM, AND SHE MAKES A SHOW OF KNOWING WHO WE ARE. I GUESS THIS IS HER WAY OF LETTING RAY KNOW THAT IF HE PLANS TO KILL US AND CARVE US INTO EASILY DISPOSED OF LITTLE PIECES, THERE WILL BE AT LEAST ONE PERSON WHO CAN IDENTIFY HIM TO THE COPS.

RAY'S WIFE IS SITTING IN THE FRONT SEAT. HE'S JUST PICKED HER UP FROM WORK, AND SHE'S LESS THAN TOTALLY PSYCHED TO BE MAKING AN UNEXPECTED ROAD TRIP TO LAFAYETTE. I'M NOT SURE WHY SHE'S JOINING US. MAYBE RAY WAS AS WORRIED TO BE CARVED UP INTO LITTLE PIECES AS WE WERE.

IT TURNS OUT THAT RAY IS A GOOD GUY. WHILE TED SLEEPS, AND RAY'S WIFE STARES ICILY OUT THE SIDE WINDOW, RAY TELLS ME

ABOUT THE BEST PLACES TO PLAY BINGO IN FT. WAYNE, AND ABOUT HIS FAVORITE CASINOS IN MISSOURI. HE TELLS ME HE GOT INTO A LOT OF TROUBLE AS A TEENAGER, WHICH IS HOW HE GOT INVOLVED IN "TEEN CHALLENGE," A BIBLE-BASED PROGRAM FOR TROUBLED YOUTH. THE IDEA OF TEEN CHALLENGE IS THAT YOU CAN TURN A BAD KID AROUND IF YOU MAKE HIM SPEND A LOT OF TIME IN THE MIDDLE OF THE WOODS. "NOTHIN' LIKE BEING CHASED BY A BEAR TO GET YOUR HEAD STRAIGHT," RAY SAYS.

IT TAKES AROUND AN HOUR TO GET TO LAFAYETTE. AS WE CROSS THE WABASH RIVER, RAY'S WIFE FINALLY SPEAKS. "RIVER? HAH! IT'S NOT A RIVER, OKAY? IT'S A FREAKING

CREEK!"

THAT NIGHT, WE CRASH AT SHEILA AND FRANK'S PLACE. SHEILA IS A UNITARIAN AND SHE ORGANIZED MY MOVIE SCREENING. FRANK PERFORMS A LITTLE KLEZMER PIANO BEFORE SAYING GOODNIGHT. TED AND I SLEEP IN THE DEN, SURROUNDED BY FOUR COMPUTERS, A FEW MICROSCOPES, A VOLTMETER, AND PILES OF "MAGIC - THE MAGAZINE FOR MAGICIANS."

08/29/06

WE SPEND A COUPLE DAYS IN LAFAYETTE. THE SCREENING AT PURDUE IS A BIG SUCCESS THANKS TO SHEILA. NOW TED IS HEADING BACK TO PHILLY. HE CRAMS HIS BIKE INTO A BIKE BOX, THEN CRAMS HIS BIKE BOX INTO THE BACK SEAT OF AN A-1 CAB. WE

HUG, AND THEN HE'S GONE, AND I'M ALL BY MYSELF.

I RIDE OUT OF LAFAYETTE AND GET LUNCH IN AN OLD DOWNTOWN HOTEL IN ATTICA. A GRILLED CHEESE SANDWICH WITH A SLICED DILL PICKLE ON THE SIDE. IT'S MORE THAN A LUNCH ORDER. IT'S A MAGIC SPELL THAT CONJURES UP EVERY OTHER GRILLED CHEESE SANDWICH I'VE EATEN AND ALL THE SLEEPY LITTLE TOWNS WHERE I'VE EATEN THEM. IF I COULD COLLECT THOSE FAR FLUNG LUNCHTIMES TOGETHER AND CALL THEM MY LIFE, THEN I COULD SAY I LIVED A PRETTY GOOD LIFE.

I SPEND THE REST OF THE DAY ON MY BIKE. CORN AND SOYBEANS. SOYBEANS AND CORN. JUST PAST A FARM HOUSE, A BIG DOG WITH BAD INTENTIONS

COMES RUNNING AT ME FULL TILT. I'M TOO TIRED TO MAKE A BREAK FOR IT. SO I RAISE MYSELF UP ON MY PEDALS AND I SUMMON UP ALL THE FURY OF A BIKE RIDER WHO'S BEEN CHASED ACROSS FOUR STATES BY DOGS. "NO!" I SCREAM. THERE'S SOMETHING IN MY VOICE, I GUESS. SOME PITCH THAT THE DOG RECOGNIZES. AND LIKE A DOG IN A CARTOON, IT SKIDS TO A STOP — SCREECHING TIRES, A CLOUD OF DUST, THE WORKS. THEN IT STANDS THERE, STUNNED, AS I RIDE AWAY. LATER, I'LL TELL LJR ABOUT THIS. "YOU FOUND YOUR DOG VOICE," SHE'LL SAY.

I CROSS THE BORDER INTO ILLINOIS, AND THINK THE SAME THOUGHT I ALWAYS THINK AT THESE STATE LINES: I CAN'T BELIEVE I'VE MADE IT THIS FAR. THERE'S A

CAMPGROUND AT KICKAPOO STATE PARK, SO THAT'S WHERE I AIM, RESIGNED TO ANOTHER DINNER OF PEANUT BUTTER POWER BARS AND LUKEWARM WATER. BUT IT TURNS OUT THERE'S A SNACK BAR AT THE PARK, AND IT'S OPEN, AND THEY HAVE VEGGIE BURGERS AND HOMEMADE APPLE CRISP. I SIT DOWN AT A TABLE, THE ONLY CUSTOMER IN THE PLACE. REMINDED ONCE AGAIN THAT THE DIFFERENCE BETWEEN A GOOD LIFE AND A NOT-SO-GOOD LIFE IS MOSTLY JUST A MATTER OF LUCK.

THE PARK HAS 40 TENT SITES, AND EVERY ONE OF THEM IS EMPTY. I TELL MYSELF IT'S OKAY. THAT TONIGHT, I'LL SLEEP LIKE A BABY EVEN THOUGH I'M ALL ALONE IN THE WOODS. AROUND MIDNIGHT,

MY CELL PHONE WAKES ME UP. THERE'S A VOICEMAIL FROM RENATO. IT SOUNDS LIKE HE'S CALLING FROM A NOISY BAR.

"HI BILL," HE SAYS. "IT WAS A GOOD TRIP. BUT I WAS THINKING ABOUT IT. NEXT TRIP, TED SHOULD BRING HIS OWN TENT."

NOW THAT I'M AWAKE, I CAN'T GET BACK TO SLEEP. EVERY RUSTLING LEAF OR SNAPPING TWIG IS A KNIFE-WIELDING SERIAL KILLER OR A HUNGRY GRIZZLY BEAR. I GIVE UP, AND HEAD FOR THE BATH HOUSE, WHERE I FALL ASLEEP ON A LITTLE BENCH IN ONE OF THE SHOWERS. IT'S NO WORSE THAN SLEEPING ON A GREYHOUND BUS, I DECIDE; AN OVERNIGHT TRIP IN A SHOWER STALL.

08/30/06

RIDING THROUGH ILLINOIS IS LIKE RIDING THROUGH INDIANA. EVERY FIELD IS FULL OF CORN OR SOYBEANS. THESE AREN'T FARMS, I DECIDE, BUT EXTENSIONS OF THE FACTORY FLOOR, SUPPLYING THE INGREDIENTS FOR CORN ETHANOL, HIGH-FRUCTOSE CORN SYRUP, SOY-BASED PAINT STRIPPERS AND NEWSPAPER INK. AN INDUSTRIAL LANDSCAPE DISGUISED AS A GRANT WOOD PAINTING.

I RIDE INTO URBANA, ILLINOIS, WHERE I SHOW MY MOVIE AT THE LOCAL COLLEGE. THEN I HEAD TO THE FOOD CO-OP AND PIG OUT. BARBECUED TOFU! VEGAN PIZZA! CHERRY TARTS AND APPLE CAKE! THIS IS WHY PEOPLE GO ON FASTS. NOT BECAUSE IT RESULTS IN SOME KIND OF MENTAL CLARITY OR

SPIRITUAL TRANSFORMATION, BUT BECAUSE ALL YOUR FAVORITE FOODS TASTE A MILLION TIMES BETTER WHEN YOU'VE BEEN DEPRIVED OF THEM FOR A LONG TIME.

09/01/06

IT'S SEPTEMBER. I'VE BEEN ON THE ROAD FOR A MONTH. A GIRL NAMED RONNI OFFERS ME A LIFT TO SPRINGFIELD. I'VE GOT A SCREENING THERE TONIGHT, SO I GRATEFULLY ACCEPT. RONNI DRIVES FAST, COVERING THE 80 MILES IN NO TIME. CAR TIME. COMPRESSED. BLURRY. A SMEAR OF MINUTES AND MILE MARKERS. NOT LIKE BIKE TIME WITH ITS SLOW UNRAVELING, LIKE THE PLOT OF A FAT MYSTERY NOVEL THAT TAKES THE WHOLE SUMMER TO READ.

THE ABRAHAM LINCOLN UNITARIAN

UNIVERSALIST CHURCH IS ON THE OUTSKIRTS OF TOWN, SITTING ON A PARCEL OF LAND THAT'S BEEN CARVED OUT OF A CORNFIELD.

I MEET JACK KRIEL THERE, THE GUY WHO ARRANGED THE SCREENING. HE CHECKS OUT MY BIKE, AND TELLS ME ABOUT HIS OWN BIKE ADVENTURE BACK IN THE 70'S, WHEN HE RODE ACROSS THE COUNTRY WITH HIS BUDDY JIM.

"WE DIDN'T HAVE TENTS," HE TELLS ME, "JUST A COUPLE OF BEATER BIKES."

"WHERE'D YOU SLEEP?" I ASK.

"ON THE GROUND. SOMETIMES IN THE CITY JAIL."

I SHOW MY MOVIE ON A TINY TV IN THE BACK OF THE CHURCH. THE AUDIENCE PLUNKS DOWN ON A

COUPLE COUCHES. OLD LADY ACTIVISTS AND OLD GUY RADICALS. ONE GUY RIDES TO THE SHOW ON HIS BIKE. HE TELLS ME HE'S PLANNING A BIG RIDE FROM SOUTH AMERICA TO ALASKA, THEN ACROSS THE BERING STRAIT AND ALL THE WAY TO INDIA.

AFTER THE SHOW, JACK AND HIS WIFE PENNY TAKE ME BACK TO THEIR PLACE. IT'S LATE, BUT JACK COOKS UP A VEGGIE STIR FRY AND OPENS A BOTTLE OF WINE. AFTER DINNER, I GO TO SLEEP IN THEIR GROWN-UP DAUGHTER'S BED UNDER HER OLD CHARLIE BROWN SHEETS.

09/02/06

IN THE MORNING, JACK AND PENNY FEED ME BREAKFAST THEN DRIVE

ME OUT TO THE HEAD OF THE INTERURBAN TRAIL, A RAIL TRAIL THAT WILL TAKE ME OUT OF SPRINGFIELD. PENNY MAKES ME POSE WITH MY BIKE THEN SNAPS MY PICTURE.

"YOU'LL WANT TO REMEMBER THIS SOMEDAY," SHE SAYS.

I ZIGZAG ACROSS SOUTHERN ILLINOIS. FARM DOGS MARK THE MILES. JUST OUTSIDE CARLINVILLE, AN OLD BLACK AND WHITE MUTT LOPES BEHIND ME IN A SLOW SPEED PURSUIT. HE'S AN OLD DOG WHOSE CHASING DAYS ARE BEHIND HIM. I SLOW DOWN A LITTLE, JUST TO GIVE HIM A CHANCE.

I FOLLOW THE REMNANTS OF OLD ROUTE 66. A VESTIGIAL ROAD. SOMETIMES IT'S ROUGH AND ALL CRACKS WITH A FADING YELLOW LINE DOWN THE MIDDLE. SOMETIMES

IT'S BARELY EVEN A ROAD. IN THAYER, IT'S AN OVERGROWN STRETCH OF ASPHALT NO WIDER THAN A SIDEWALK. THEN EVEN THAT CRUMBLES AWAY TILL ROUTE 66 IS BARELY A TRACE THAT CUTS ACROSS SOMEBODY'S FRONT LAWN. THE GUY WHO OWNS THAT LAWN IS MOWING IT WITH HIS SIT-DOWN MOWER. HE LOOKS SURPRISED WHEN I RIDE BY AND WAVE.

09/03/06

I WAKE UP EARLY, THANKS TO THE DUDES IN THE MOTEL ROOM NEXT TO MINE WHO ROLL IN AT 4 AM AND KEEP THE PARTY GOING TILL 7. I MAKE A POINT OF SLAMMING MY DOOR AS I LEAVE.

I ROLL THROUGH A SUNNY MORNING PAST FIELDS LINED WITH A PRECISE RASTER OF SOYBEAN PLANTS; FIELDS PLOWED BY ROBOT TRACTORS GUIDED

BY SATELLITES AND LASER BEAMS. TO MY EXPANDING "LIST OF THINGS I'M OFFICIALLY SICK OF" — A LIST THAT INCLUDES ENERGY BARS, FARM DOGS, AND CORN — I ADD GENETICALLY MODIFIED SOYBEANS.

ALL MORNING, THERE ARE DOGS. BIG FLUFFY ONES AND LITTLE YAPPY ONES. IT'S EXHAUSTING TO GET AMBUSHED EVERY HALF MILE. COMBAT FATIGUE KICKS IN. I TRY OUT A NEW TRICK SOME CYCLIST SUGGESTED, SQUIRTING THE DOGS WITH MY WATER BOTTLE. IT WORKS PRETTY WELL. DEFINITELY BETTER THAN MY "DOG VOICE," WHICH IS HARD TO SUMMON WHEN YOU'RE STRUGGLING OVER HILLS AND CAN BARELY CATCH YOUR BREATH. THE DOG VOICE DEPENDS ON A CONVINCING PERFORMANCE, AND DOGS ARE A TOUGH CROWD. THEY

CAN TELL WHEN YOUR HEART ISN'T IN IT.

I MISS A TURN AND WIND UP IN MOUNT OLIVE, ILLINOIS. IT'S THE DAY BEFORE LABOR DAY, SO I FIGURE IT'S MEANT TO BE. MOUNT OLIVE IS WHERE MOTHER JONES IS BURIED. HER GRAVE IS IN THE UNION MINERS' CEMETERY, MARKED BY A GRANITE PILLAR AND GUARDED BY A COUPLE BRONZE MINERS, ONE HOLDING A PICK-AXE AND THE OTHER A SLEDGE HAMMER. A COUPLE MINERS YOU WOULDN'T WANT TO MESS WITH. MOTHER JONES WAS BORN IN IRELAND, BUT SHE WAS A LABOR ACTIVIST AND SHE WANTED TO BE BURIED HERE IN MOUNT OLIVE, ALONGSIDE THE COAL MINERS WHO WERE KILLED IN THE 1898 "VIRDEN

MASSACRE." UNION MINERS WERE ON STRIKE AT THE CHICAGO-VIRDEN COAL COMPANY. WHEN THE MINE OWNERS SENT IN STRIKE BREAKERS, THINGS GOT UGLY. THE MINE GUARDS STARTED SHOOTING AT THE STRIKERS, THEN THE STRIKERS SHOT BACK. A LOT OF PEOPLE GOT KILLED. THE STRIKE BREAKERS, BY THE WAY, WERE POOR AFRICAN-AMERICANS ESCAPING THE JIM CROW SOUTH. IT WAS A PRETTY SMART STRATEGY, AS FAR AS THE MINE OWNERS WERE CONCERNED. GOT A CLASS WAR ON YOUR HANDS? THEN START A RACE WAR AMONG YOUR OPPONENTS.

I'M CLOSING IN ON ST. LOUIS NOW. IN EDWARDSVILLE, I FIND A PLACE THAT MAKES FALAFEL WRAPS. I EAT ONE. THEN I EAT ANOTHER. A SNAKE MEAL. THAT'S WHAT LJR CALLS IT. EATING WHILE THE

EATING IS GOOD, LIKE WHEN A SNAKE EATS AN ELEPHANT AND SPENDS THE NEXT MONTH DIGESTING IT.

I'M ON THE GOSHEN TRAIL NOW. IT'S PART OF THE 100-MILE MADISON COUNTY TRANSIT TRAIL SYSTEM. FOR THE LAST TWENTY YEARS, THIS COUNTY JUST EAST OF ST. LOUIS HAS BEEN CONVERTING OLD RAIL ROAD CORRIDORS INTO TOP-KNOTCH BIKE TRAILS. MADISON COUNTY PROBABLY HAS ONE OF THE BEST COMMUTER BIKE TRAIL NETWORKS IN THE WHOLE COUNTRY. I TAKE THE GOSHEN TRAIL TO THE SCHOOL HOUSE TRAIL, THEN HOP UP ONTO A LEVEE. 1000 MILES FROM D.C. AND THERE IT IS. THE MISSISSIPPI RIVER. HOT DAMN.

09/04/06

I WAKE UP WITH A SORE THROAT. EVERY BREATH I'VE BREATHED OUT DURING THE NIGHT HAS CONDENSED

ABOVE ME ON THE FABRIC OF MY TENT. WHEN I MOVE, A LITTLE STORM OF EXHALED BREATHS SHOWERS DOWN.

I'M STAYING AT A CAMPGROUND IN GRANITE CITY, ACROSS THE RIVER FROM ST. LOUIS. GRANITE CITY IS A FORLORN PLACE. TRUCK STOPS. ABANDONED FACTORIES. IT'S A GOOD PLACE TO DUMP THINGS YOU DON'T WANT PEOPLE TO KNOW YOU'RE DUMPING. OVER THE RIVER IS ST. LOUIS, A CITY THAT HAS SEEN BETTER DAYS. PARTS OF IT ARE BURNED OUT, DETROIT-STYLE. THERE ARE NEIGH-BORHOODS WHERE PHEASANTS AND RACCOONS NOW OUTNUMBER THE TAX PAYERS BY A WIDE MARGIN. BUT DESPITE ALL THAT (AND PARTLY BECAUSE OF ALL THAT), IT'S A GREAT PLACE TO RIDE A BIKE. I MENTIONED

THE COMMUTER TRAILS IN ILLINOIS. BUT THERE ARE ALSO TRAILS ON TOP OF THE LEVEES ALONG THE RIVER, AND THERE'S EVEN A RIVER BRIDGE DEDICATED TO WALKERS AND BIKERS. NOT SOME DINKY BRIDGE, EITHER, BUT THE OLD ROUTE 66 BRIDGE, A MAGNIFICENT STEEL TRUSS THING. THE CHAIN OF ROCKS BRIDGE - THAT'S OFFICIALLY WHAT IT'S CALLED. IT'S NAMED FOR SOME ROCKS IN THE MIDDLE OF THE RIVER THAT WERE A SERIOUS NAVIGATIONAL HAZARD. IT WAS ABANDONED DECADES AGO WHEN THEY BUILT THE INTER-STATE BRIDGE JUST UP-RIVER. THE BRIDGE SURVIVED BECAUSE ST. LOUIS WAS TOO POOR TO KNOCK IT DOWN. THEN, IN THE LATE 1990'S, THE MOST FANTASTICALLY IMPROBABLE THING HAPPENED. A NOT-FOR-PROFIT RAISED ENOUGH CASH TO RESTORE

THE BRIDGE AND TURN IT INTO A CROSSING FOR BIKES AND PEDES-TRIANS. AND JUST LIKE THAT, ST. LOUIS GAINED ONE OF THE RADDEST CYCLING ATTRACTIONS ON THE ENTIRE PLANET.

THE BRIDGE DOESN'T SHOOT STRAIGHT ACROSS THE MISSISSIPPI. INSTEAD, IT HAS A 20-DEGREE KINK IN IT, RIGHT IN THE MIDDLE. SOMEBODY TELLS ME IT'S LIKE THAT BECAUSE OF THE GEOLOGY OF THE RIVER BED. SOMEBODY ELSE SAYS IT WAS TO MAKE NAVIGATING AROUND IT EASIER FOR BARGES. I DECIDE IT'S JUST ANOTHER MYSTERY, PART OF THE SAME HAPPY MAGIC THAT RESCUED THE BRIDGE FROM CARS AND COLLAPSE AND DELIVERED IT TO THE BIKE RIDERS.

TWO LITTLE CASTLES SIT IN THE RIVER JUST DOWN STREAM FROM THE

BRIDGE. A BIRD WATCHER NOTICES ME LOOKING AT THEM.
"THOSE ARE WATER INTAKES FOR THE CITY'S DRINKING WATER," HE TELLS ME. I LOOK AT THE MUDDY WATER COURSING UNDER THE BRIDGE.
"PEOPLE DRINK THIS WATER?" I ASK. THE GUY NODS. WHAT I DON'T KNOW THEN IS THAT DURING A BLIND TASTE TEST CONDUCTED BY THE U.S. CONFERENCE OF MAYORS IN 2007, ST. LOUIS WILL WIN THE VOTE FOR THE BEST TASTING TAP WATER IN THE U.S.

LATER ON, I MEET MIKE OVER BY WASHINGTON U. MIKE IS TED'S PAL, THE SAME MIKE WHO DROVE TED TO PITTSBURGH THREE WEEKS AGO. I DIDN'T KNOW IT, BUT AS MIKE WAS DRIVING BACK TO PHILLY, HE WAS HATCHING A PLAN TO DITCH HIS

JOB AND JOIN UP WITH THE BIKE RIDE. NOW HERE HE IS, WITH A FANCY CANONDALE THAT HE BOUGHT FROM A COLLEGE PROFESSOR WHO WAS MOVING TO PERU.

WHILE WE POKE AROUND LOOKING FOR A PLACE TO GET DINNER, I TELL MIKE ABOUT THE CHAIN OF ROCKS BRIDGE, HOW COOL IT IS, AND HOW HE CAN CHECK IT OUT ON OUR WAY TO THE CAMPGROUND. THEN I REMEMBER SOMETHING. THE BRIDGE HAS GATES. AND THE GATES ARE LOCKED AT SUNSET. I LOOK AT THE SUN.

"UH, MIKE," I SAY, "WE KIND OF HAVE TO RUN."

WE ZIP DOWN TO THE ST. LOUIS ARCH, AND SPEED ALONG THE RIVER FRONT TRAIL. THEN THE SUN SETS. IT'S TOTALLY DARK BY THE TIME WE GET TO THE BRIDGE, BUT LUCKY

FOR US, THE GATE IS STILL OPEN. WE RUN INTO A COP MIDWAY ACROSS. HE'S ALREADY LOCKED THE GATE ON THE ILLINOIS SIDE, BUT AGREES TO TURN AROUND AND OPEN IT FOR US. "YOU BOYS BE CAREFUL," HE SAYS AS WE ROLL INTO ILLINOIS. THIS STRIKES MIKE AND ME AS A QUAINT, COPPISH THING TO SAY. THEN AGAIN, WE DON'T KNOW ABOUT THE MURDERS.

ONE NIGHT BACK IN 1991, A COUPLE TEENAGED SISTERS AND THEIR COUSIN WERE HANGING OUT ON THE BRIDGE. BACK THEN, IT WAS STILL ABANDONED AND DERELICT, SO MUCH SO THAT IT DOUBLED AS THE BRIDGE INTO MANHATTAN IN THE MOVIE "ESCAPE FROM NEW YORK." IT WAS A GHOST BRIDGE, WHICH MUST HAVE

MADE IT IRRESISTIBLE TO TEENAGERS. UNFORTUNATELY, A GROUP OF BAD MEN WERE ALSO ON THE BRIDGE THAT NIGHT. THEY ROBBED THE TEENAGERS AND PUSHED THEM OFF THE BRIDGE. ONLY THE COUSIN SURVIVED.

MIKE AND I FOLLOW THE ROAD OFF THE BRIDGE AND ON TO CHOUTEAU ISLAND, A LITTLE SPIT OF LAND BETWEEN THE MISSISS-IPPI RIVER AND THE SHIP CANAL. THE ISLAND IS COVERED WITH SOME SCRUBBY WOODS. AT NIGHT, IT'S PITCH DARK, AND THE LITTLE ROAD WE'RE ON IS EMPTY. AS WE RIDE, WE DISCUSS BIKE LIGHTS: HOW SOMETIMES YOU WANT CARS TO SEE YOU, AND SOME-TIMES YOU DON'T. WE DECIDE TO RIDE WITH OUR BIKE LIGHTS OFF.

HALFWAY ACROSS THE ISLAND, WE SEE SOME HEADLIGHTS COMING TOWARD US. BEFORE WE CAN PULL OVER, THE LIGHTS VEER OFF INTO THE WOODS. A MINUTE LATER, WE HEAR A POP-POP-POP.

"ARE THOSE GUNSHOTS?" I ASK MIKE.

"I THINK THOSE ARE GUNSHOTS," MIKE REPLIES.

WE PICK UP THE PACE, WHICH ISN'T SO EASY WHEN YOU'RE RIDING WITHOUT LIGHTS. FINALLY, WE GET TO THE BRIDGE OVER THE SHIP CANAL, AND RIDE TO THE WAFFLE HOUSE IN GRANITE CITY. WE ORDER PECAN WAFFLES AND BLACK TEA. I MAKE A TOAST.

"WELCOME TO THE BIKE TOUR, MIKE!" I SAY.

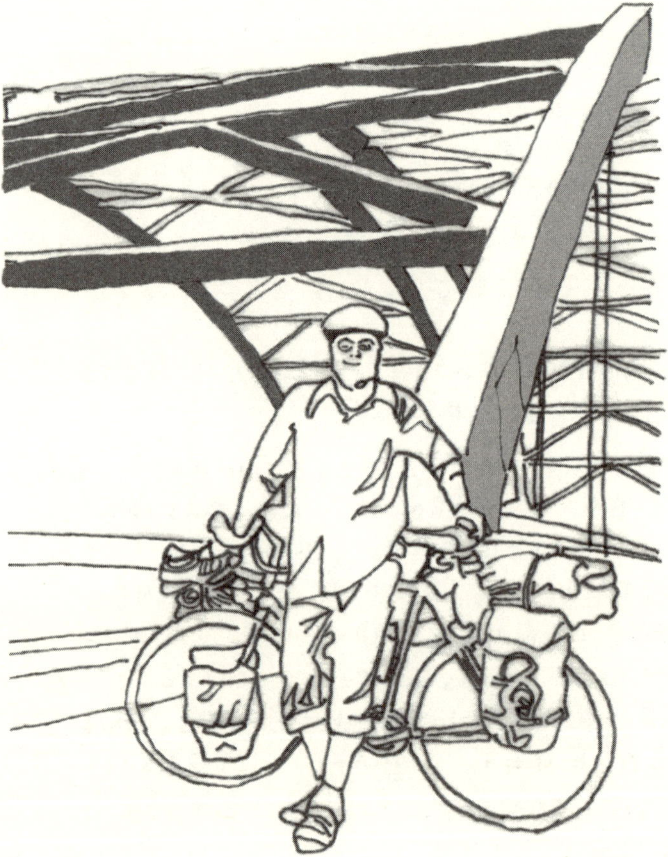

09/05/06

I TRY TO REMEMBER WHAT LEWIS AND CLARK DID WHEN THEY GOT SICK. IT SEEMS LIKE THEY MADE A LOT OF TINCTURES TO LOOSEN THEIR BOWELS. ONE OF HISTORY'S GREAT TRAVEL ACCOUNTS, "THE DIARY OF LEWIS AND CLARK," IS RIDDLED WITH CONSTIPATION. MY PROBLEM IS A BAD COLD.

MIKE AND I SPLIT UP FOR THE DAY. MIKE HEADS INTO ST. LOUIS TO TAKE A LOOK AROUND, AND I RIDE UP THE LEVEE TO ALTON, ILLINOIS, TO SHOW MY MOVIE TO THE UNITARIANS UP THERE.

ALTON IS AN OLD RIVER TOWN THAT SITS ON THE HILLY BLUFFS ABOVE THE MISSISSIPPI. IT'S FAMOUS FOR BEING ONE OF THE MOST HAUNTED TOWNS IN AMERICA, AND THE FIRST UNITARIAN CHURCH IS

SUPPOSED TO BE ONE OF THE MOST HAUNTED BUILDINGS IN TOWN.

I CALL BETH, MY CONTACT, AND WE ARRANGE TO MEET IN FRONT OF THE CHURCH. WHEN I GET THERE, SHE'S NOT AROUND. THEN I HEAR SOMEONE CALLING MY NAME FROM THE BOTTOM OF THE HILL THAT THE CHURCH IS PERCHED ON. IT'S BETH, STANDING NEXT TO HER SMASHED UP CAR. SHE TELLS ME SHE'D PARKED IT ON THE STREET IN FRONT OF THE CHURCH. AS SHE WALKED AWAY, IT BEGAN ROLLING DOWN THE HILL. IT PICKED UP ENOUGH SPEED TO SMASH THROUGH THE WALL OF A PARKING GARAGE. THE CAR IS TOTALED.

"I JUST DON'T UNDERSTAND HOW IT HAPPENED," BETH SAYS.

"GHOSTS!" I THINK TO MYSELF.

DESPITE THE WRECK, BETH INSISTS THAT THE SHOW MUST GO ON.

ONCE AGAIN, THE AUDIENCE IS A POSSE OF AWESOME UNITARIANS: HIPPIES, OLD LEFTIES, AND SOME RECENT IMMIGRANTS FROM MEXICO. AFTER THE SCREENING, EVERYONE SITS AROUND DRINKING CHURCH COFFEE AND TALKING ABOUT HOW THE RICH ARE FUCKING THE REST OF US OVER. I DECIDE THAT ONCE THIS BIKE TOUR IS OVER, I'M GOING TO BECOME A UNITARIAN.

I RIDE BACK TO GRANITE CITY ON THE LEVEE TRAIL. THERE'S A FULL MOON, SO I SWITCH OFF MY BIKE LIGHT AND COAST THROUGH THE MOONLIGHT. THE LEVEE IS HIGH, MAYBE 15 OR 20 FEET. WHEN YOU RIDE UP THERE AT NIGHT, IT FEELS LIKE YOU'RE FLYING, SECRET AND

STEALTHY, OVER THE FLOOD PLAIN.

09/06/06

BIKING INTO ST. LOUIS IS EASY, BUT BIKING OUT IS A TRICK. WE PACK UP THE TENTS AND CROSS THE BIG BRIDGE ONE LAST TIME, AND WE RIDE THE RIVER TRAIL INTO TOWN. THE RIVER TRAIL DOESN'T MESS AROUND, BUT TAKES US RIGHT THROUGH THE MIDDLE OF BARGES BEING LOADED AND BOX CARS BEING HUMPED. IT'S THE BEST KIND OF TRAIL, ONE THAT MAKES YOU FEEL LIKE YOU'RE SNEAKING WHERE YOU SHOULDN'T BE SNEAKING.

WE ROLL UP MARKET STREET, GAWKING LIKE A COUPLE COUNTRY BUMPKINS WHO JUST HOPPED OFF A PADDLE BOAT. THERE'S THE ART DECO WORLD WAR ONE MEMORIAL THAT'S GOT A MUSEUM DEDICATED TO MACHINE

GUNS AND LAND MINES INSIDE. NOT FAR FROM THERE IS THE VAST ROMANESQUE FORTRESS THAT HOUSED UNION STATION, ONCE THE BUSIEST TRAIN STATION ON THE PLANET. ON MARKET STREET, YOU CAN PRETEND THAT ST. LOUIS IS THE BIGGEST, BADDEST CITY IN THE MIDWEST, AND CHICAGO IS JUST A COWTOWN.

THERE'S NO EASY WAY OUT OF ST. LOUIS, AS FAR AS MIKE AND I CAN TELL. SO WE DUST OFF THE "PITTSBURGH STRATEGY": FIND A CITY BUS THAT HEADS WEST, AND TAKE IT TO THE LAST STOP. SOMEHOW, WE PICK THE #32 LOCAL, WHICH MAKES A THOUSAND STOPS BEFORE IT DUMPS US ALONG-SIDE A DRAINAGE DITCH ON THE OUTSKIRTS OF THE CITY. MIKE AND I STAND ON THE SIDE OF THE ROAD,

A LITTLE STUNNED, FEELING LIKE WE JUST GOT RUN OUT OF TOWN ON A RAIL.

MY COLD TAKES A TURN FOR THE WORSE. WE CHECK IN TO A MOTEL 6 AND I SLEEP FOR THE NEXT 14 HOURS, SWEATING MY WAY THROUGH TWO T-SHIRTS AND A PAIR OF SHORTS, LIKE A MAN WITH A TROPICAL FEVER. LEWIS AND CLARK AREN'T THERE TO PLY ME WITH POULTICES, BUT MIKE BRINGS ME A PLATE OF PASTA FROM OLIVE GARDEN.

09/07/06

WE RIDE THROUGH CREVE COEUR PARK, FRENCH FOR "BROKEN HEART." THE PARK'S LOGO IS A LITTLE RED HEART THAT'S CRACKED IN TWO. THEN ACROSS THE MISSOURI RIVER AND ONTO THE KATY TRAIL, A 240 MILE RAIL TRAIL THAT WILL

TAKE US CLEAR ACROSS MISSOURI. THE TRAIL GOT ITS NAME FROM THE "K-T" PART OF THE M-K-T RAILROAD THAT USED TO OWN THE TRACKS: THE MISSOURI-KANSAS-TEXAS. THE KATY IS THE LONGEST RAIL TRAIL IN THE U.S., AT LEAST UNTIL THEY FINISH THE COWBOY TRAIL UP IN NEBRASKA WHICH WILL CLOCK IN AT 320 MILES.

FOR THE REST OF THE DAY, WE RIDE ALONG NEXT TO THE MISSOURI RIVER, STOPPING NOW AND THEN TO READ THE HISTORICAL PLAQUES THAT DESCRIBE LEWIS AND CLARK'S PROGRESS AS THEY FLOATED WEST ON THE RIVER, AND GENERALLY GLOATING THAT WE'RE TOTALLY DUSTIN' THOSE FOOLS.

WE STOP FOR THE NIGHT IN MARTHASVILLE AT CHOO CHOO'S FROZEN CUSTARD AND CAMPGROUND. THE PLACE IS CLOSED FOR THE SEASON,

BUT WE FIND A PHONE NUMBER. WE CALL IT. THE LADY WHO ANSWERS TELLS US TO PICK A TENT SITE— THERE ARE FIVE TOTAL— AND TO LEAVE 5 BUCKS TUCKED UNDER THE TAKE-OUT WINDOW OF THE CUSTARD STAND.

WE WALK INTO TOWN AND FIND A BAR CALLED DEB'S. DEB IS THE ONLY PERSON IN THE PLACE. DURING THE DAY, SHE WORKS AT A HOME FOR THE MENTALLY HANDICAPPED. AT NIGHT, SHE RUNS THE BAR. THERE'S A LOT TO ADMIRE IN THAT BAR. THE WARPED WOODEN FLOORS. THE OLD DART BOARDS. DEB TELLS US ABOUT THE FLOOD OF '93 WHEN THE BAR FILLED UP WITH MUD, AND SHE WARNS US TO WATCH OUT FOR THE LOCAL COP WHO'S ON A POWER TRIP, AND WHO LIES ABOUT MAKING

DRUG BUSTS AND HAVING NIGHT VISION GOGGLES. SHE TELLS US ABOUT THE BIG EXCITEMENT A COUPLE YEARS AGO WHEN THEY WERE HAVING A TRACTOR PULL COMPETITION, AND ON THE WAY TO THE EVENT, ONE OF THE TRACTORS GOT HIT BY A CAR. THE TRACTOR DRIVER DIED, AND THE GUY WHO HIT HIM WAS HIS BEST FRIEND. DEB IS GENEROUS WITH HER TOWN'S SECRETS, AND WHEN WE FINALLY SAY GOODNIGHT, WE FEEL LIKE HONORARY LOCALS.

IT'S LATE WHEN WE GET BACK TO OUR TENTS. JUST BEFORE I FALL ASLEEP, THE LOCAL COP ROLLS BY. HE HITS US WITH HIS SEARCH LIGHT, THEN DRIVES AWAY.

"WHY DOES HE NEED A LIGHT?" MIKE WHISPERS FROM HIS TENT. "CAN'T HE JUST USE HIS NIGHT VISION GOGGLES?"

09/08/06

BREAKFAST IS A PEANUT BUTTER GRANOLA BAR AND A CAN OF DEL MONTE FRUIT COCKTAIL IN HEAVY SYRUP. EVERY 5 OR 10 MILES, WE PASS A HISTORICAL MARKER THAT LETS US KNOW HOW THINGS ARE GOING WITH LEWIS AND CLARK: WHERE THEY CAMPED, AND WHAT THEY ATE, AND WHO THEY MET. MYSTERIOUSLY, THEY DIDN'T MEET DANIEL BOONE, EVEN THOUGH THEY STOPPED AT THE SETTLEMENT HE FOUNDED AND WHERE HE WAS STILL LIVING. WAS HE SNUBBING THEM? WAS HE CONSTIPATED? HISTORY IS SILENT ON THE MATTER.

WE TAKE A DETOUR OFF THE TRAIL AND CROSS THE RIVER INTO HERMANN, A TOWN FOUNDED BY GERMANS THAT'S NOW A KIND OF WEEKEND GETAWAY KNOWN FOR ITS OKTOBERFEST AND ITS HISTORIC

DOWNTOWN. MIKE AND I WIND UP AT A MEXICAN PLACE FOR LUNCH. IN RETROSPECT, IT SEEMS LIKE AN OBVIOUSLY BAD IDEA TO GET MEXICAN FOOD IN A GERMAN THEME TOWN. I ORDER A VEGGIE FAJITA, WHICH ARRIVES DRENCHED IN A THICK AMBER GREASE FLECKED WITH BITS OF HAMBURGER. MIKE'S ENCHILADAS LOOK LIKE THE SCENE OF A MURDER-SUICIDE. LUNCH IS BRIEF.

BACK ON THE TRAIL, WE HEAD FOR TEBBETTS. THAT'S WHERE CATHY LIVES, ONE OF THE UNITARIANS WHO SET UP MY MOVIE SCREENING IN JEFFERSON CITY TOMORROW. TEBBETTS IS A HAUL. PRETTY SOON IT'S DARK, AND THE KATY TRAIL IS A FAINT TRACE IN THE MOONLIGHT. I SNAP ON MY BIKE LIGHT AND FOLLOW MIKE, WHO'S JUST A COUPLE STRIPES OF REFLECTIVE TAPE FLOATING IN THE

DARKNESS AHEAD.

09/09/06 – 09/10/06

THE MOVIE SCREENING IN JEFF CITY IS AT 9 AM ON A SATURDAY MORNING. TOO EARLY FOR THE UNITARIANS, EVEN. ATTENDANCE IS SPARSE. IT'S A LITTLE BETTER IN COLUMBIA THE NEXT NIGHT. WE SCREEN AT THE RAGTAG, A LITTLE DOWNTOWN MOVIE HOUSE. COLUMBIA IS A COLLEGE TOWN: AN OASIS OF SMOOTHIE SHOPS AND BAGEL JOINTS IN THE GREAT WILDERNESS OF QUICKIE MARTS AND GREASY SPOONS WHERE WE'VE BEEN SOJOURNING.

WE MEET HAPPY, WHO WORKS AT THE THEATER'S CONCESSION STAND.

SHE INVITES US TO CRASH AT THE RANCH. IT'S THE LOCAL PUNK ROCK HOUSE, A RAMBLING 1950'S RANCH HOUSE THAT THE GUY WHO STARTED RAGTAG INHERITED FROM HIS GRANDMA. NOW IT'S FULL OF PUNK ROCK KIDS SLEEPING IN ALL THE NOOKS AND CRANNIES.

MIKE TELLS ME ABOUT THE PUNK HOUSES IN PHILLY. CASTLE GRAYSKULL, AND THE LEGENDARY LESS COCK ("IT WAS TRYING TO BE MORE ABOUT THE LADIES," HE SAYS). HOUSES THAT ARE LIKE EMBASSIES OF THE COUNTRY YOU'RE FROM: THAT REPUBLIC OF DUMPSTER-DIVING, TRAIN-HOPPING, SIDEWALK-STENCILING, WHEAT-PASTING, ZINE-WRITING, BIKE-RIDING FREEGAN FREAKINESS THAT YOU'RE MORE-OR-LESS A CITIZEN OF.

HAPPY WARNS US ABOUT THE BROWN RECLUSE SPIDERS: A SMALL, HARMLESS-LOOKING SPIDER THAT LIKES TO HIDE UNDER THINGS. PILLOWS. SHEETS. SLEEPING BAGS. IF YOU'RE UNLUCKY ENOUGH TO GET STUNG BY ONE, YOU CAN EXPECT THE PART OF YOUR BODY THAT GOT STUNG TO TURN BLACK AND, AFTER A GOOD AMOUNT OF AGONIZING PAIN, FALL OFF.

"I KILLED A DOZEN OF THEM IN MY ROOM," HAPPY TELLS US BEFORE WISHING US A GOOD NIGHT.

MIKE AND I SIT IN DUMB HORROR FOR A WHILE.

"WHAT SHOULD WE DO?" MIKE FINALLY ASKS.

"MAYBE WE SHOULD PITCH OUR TENTS IN THE YARD?" I SUGGEST.

BUT IT'S LATE, AND THE YARD IS REALLY DARK. MIKE DECIDES IT'S SAFEST TO SLEEP ON THE FLOOR. HE PUSHES ALL OUR STUFF INTO THE CORNER OF THE ROOM, LEAVING A DEFENSIBLE CLEARING AROUND HIS SLEEPING BAG. I GUESS HE FIGURES THIS WILL GIVE HIM A FIGHTING CHANCE. MEANWHILE, I PULL THE COUCH APART.

"AHH!" I SCREAM.

"SPIDER?" MIKE ASKS.

"MOLDY POTATO CHIP," I SAY.

09/11/06

WE WAKE UP TO POUNDING ON THE FRONT DOOR. THE PUNK KIDS HAVEN'T PAID THE WATER BILL, AND A COUPLE GUYS WHO LOOK LIKE BOUNCERS FROM COLUMBIA'S MOST DANGEROUS BAR HAVE COME TO CUT OFF THE WATER.

MIKE AND I PACK UP AND HIT THE TRAIL. WE HAVEN'T BEEN OUT LONG WHEN WE COME ACROSS A BUFF, SWEATY DUDE WHO IS FIDDLING WITH THE REAR BRAKES OF A FANCY-LOOKING HYBRID BIKE. WE ASK HIM IF HE NEEDS A HAND.

"HI, I'M CARL EDWARDS," HE SAYS. THEN HE STANDS THERE, WAITING FOR THIS INFORMATION TO SINK IN.

MIKE AND I SMILE POLITELY.

"I'M A NASCAR DRIVER," HE SAYS.

"AH," I SAY.

CARL EDWARDS TELLS US HE LOVES THE KATY TRAIL. HE ASKS US ABOUT OUR TRIP. THEN HE GIVES US HIS CELL PHONE NUMBER.

"NEXT TIME Y'ALL ARE PASSING THROUGH COLUMBIA, GIVE ME A CALL," HE SAYS.

WE STOP FOR LUNCH AT A LITTLE DINER IN ROCHEPORT.
"CARL EDWARDS RODE THROUGH TODAY," THE GIRL AT THE REGISTER TELLS US. SHE SEEMS SORT OF STARSTRUCK. I NOTICE THERE'S A NEWSPAPER PHOTO OF CARL TACKED TO THE WALL. "GOLDEN BOY," THE CAPTION READS. MIKE NOTICES THE PHOTO, TOO. "DO YOU THINK YOU SHOULD TELL HER YOU HAVE CARL EDWARDS' PHONE NUMBER IN YOUR POCKET?" HE WHISPERS.

WE RIDE TO BOONVILLE AND CHECK INTO A DUMPY MOTEL. DINNER IS AVOCADO SANDWICHES ON PAPER PLATES THAT WE EAT OUT IN THE PARKING LOT. BEFORE I GO TO SLEEP, I COMPARE A MAP OF MISSOURI WITH A MAP OF KANSAS. MISSOURI IS ALL SQUIGGLES. KANSAS IS ALL NINETY-DEGREE ANGLES.

09/12/06

WHEN WE GO TO BED, IT'S SUMMER. WHEN WE WAKE UP, IT'S FALL. A COLD WIND IS BLOWING FROM THE NORTH. MIKE AND I DRAG OUR FEET. WE GET A FEW CUPS OF COFFEE AT TAYLOR'S BAKE SHOPPE, THEN SNOOP AROUND AN OLD RAILROAD CABOOSE DOWN BY THE TOURIST OFFICE. WHEN WE FINALLY HIT THE TRAIL, IT'S A SLOW, STEADY UPHILL GRIND AS THE RAILROAD CORRIDOR LEAVES THE MISSOURI FLOODPLAIN AND CLIMBS INTO THE BORDER LANDS OF THE OZARKS.

WE GET TO SEDALIA AND CAMP AT THE MISSOURI STATE FAIRGROUNDS. WE READ THAT THERE ARE OVER 2000 CAMPSITES, BUT TONIGHT, WE'RE THE ONLY CAMPERS. NO ONE

S AROUND AND NO ONE CHECKS US IN. MIKE AND I HEAD TO THE BATH HOUSE, A PLACE THAT'S BIG ENOUGH FOR 2000 CAMPERS TO TAKE 2000 SHOWERS AND 2000 PEES. THE SHOWERS ARE IN A DARK, ECHOEY CAVERN WITH CHOCOLATE BROWN TILES ON THE WALLS. MINERAL DEPOSIT STALACTITES HANG FROM THE CEILING.

"YOU GONNA TAKE A SHOWER?" MIKE ASKS ME.

"NAH," I SAY. "ARE YOU?"

"NAH," MIKE SAYS.

09/13/06

THE AMTRAK STATION IN SEDALIA USED TO BE THE MISSOURI PACIFIC STATION. IT WAS BUILT IN THE LATE 1800'S, BUT YOU'D NEVER KNOW IT. IN 1951, THEY LOPPED THE SECOND FLOOR OFF AND STRIPPED AWAY THE ARCHITECTURAL DETAILS,

LEAVING A LITTLE BRICK BOX BEHIND. THE PLACE IS EMPTY. NO TICKET OFFICE. JUST A PEPSI MACHINE AND A BEAT-UP PIANO. I GUESS THE PIANO IS A NOD TO SCOTT JOPLIN, WHO LIVED IN SEDALIA FOR A FEW YEARS AND WROTE HIS MAPLE LEAF RAG HERE. I PLAY A FEW NOTES. THE PIANO IS WAY OUT OF TUNE.

ED THE ANARCHIST HAS AGREED TO DRIVE DOWN FROM KANSAS CITY AND PICK US UP. UNTIL THEN, MIKE AND I HAVE A COUPLE HOURS TO KILL. I HEAD DOWNTOWN. IN THE LATE 1800'S, SEDALIA WAS BOOMING. STOCKYARDS AND RAILROADS MADE THE TOWN RICH, AND THE BUILDINGS FROM THAT ERA ARE AMAZING: BIG, RAMBLING, ASYMMETRICAL PILES OF STONE THAT ARE HAUNTED A THOUSAND TIMES OVER. WHILE I'M

ADMIRING ONE CALLED THE TRUST BUILDING, AN OLD MAN TODDLES OVER.
"THEY SHOULDA SENT FIGHTER JETS TO SHOOT 'EM DOWN," HE SAYS.
"EXCUSE ME?" I SAY.
"WHEN THEY WERE GONNA HIT THEM TOWERS. THE BAD GUYS. THEY SHOULD'VE SHOT 'EM DOWN."

DOWNTOWN SEDALIA HAS SEEN BETTER DAYS. THAT'S THE DANGER OF THESE OLD RAILROAD TOWNS. THEY CAN CONVINCE YOU THAT THINGS USED TO BE BETTER. IF YOU'RE NOT CAREFUL, THEY CAN TURN YOU INTO A SENTIMENTAL FOOL.

ED THE ANARCHIST IS A FRIEND OF A FRIEND OF LJR'S. HE SET UP OUR MOVIE SCREENING IN KANSAS CITY. IN FACT, THE REST OF OUR SCREENINGS ARE AT ANARCHIST

SPACES. THE UNITARIAN PORTION OF THE BIKE TOUR IS OVER; THE ANARCHIST PORTION HAS BEGUN.

09/14/06 – 09/17/06

THE K.C. SHOW ISN'T TILL THE 17TH, SO WE HAVE A FEW DAYS OFF. IT MAKES ME EDGY, THIS STAYING PUT. MAYBE ED SENSES THIS, BECAUSE HE OFFERS TO TAKE US ON ONE OF HIS ALL-DAY WALKS. ED IS FAMOUS FOR HIS WALKS. HE'S THE KIND OF GUY WHO THINKS NOTHING OF WALKING 40 MILES TO LAWRENCE, KANSAS TO SEE A BAND, THEN TURNING AROUND AND WALKING HOME. SO WE WALK: MID-CITY TO DOWNTOWN; UP QUALITY HILL AND DOWN TO THE BOTTOMS. WHEN WE GET BACK TO ED'S PLACE, MIKE

MAKES HIS FAKE TUNA SALAD:
A FEW CANS OF GARBANZO BEANS, CRUSHED.
SHREDDED CARROTS, SLICED CELERY
A FEW BIG SCOOPS OF VEGANAISE
DILL, PEPPER, SALT, WHATNOT
SLAP THE MIXTURE ON SOME BREAD. ADD DILL PICKLES AND A BOTTLE OF BEER ON THE SIDE.

I DON'T KEEP NOTES FOR THE NEXT COUPLE DAYS. MAYBE IT'S BECAUSE WE'VE STOPPED BIKING AND THE TRIP FEELS LIKE IT'S ON HOLD. MAYBE IT'S BECAUSE ED'S ROOMMATE'S NIGHTLY NOISY SEX HAS LEFT ME SLEEP-DEPRIVED. ANYWAY, WE SHOW THE MOVIES TO A

HANDFUL OF KC ANARCHISTS, THEN WE SAY THANKS TO ED AND HIT THE ROAD AGAIN.

09/18/06

LAWRENCE, KANSAS. ANOTHER COLLEGE TOWN, BUT I LIKE THIS ONE ALOT. MAYBE IT'S THE LIGHT. A GOLDEN, WHEAT-COLORED LIGHT. ONCE WE CROSS THE BORDER, THE COLORS SHIFT; NO LONGER THE WEEDY GREENS OF MISSOURI, BUT THE RUSSETS AND TANS OF KANSAS.

MIKE AND I RIDE TO SOLIDARITY, THE ANARCHIST SPACE WHERE WE'RE SCREENING THE MOVIES. THEY'VE GOT FREE INTERNET AND A LENDING LIBRARY OF RADICAL BOOKS. THE PLACE IS TIDY AND WELL-ORGANIZED, WHICH MAKES ME THINK

THAT AFTER MESSIER ANARCHISTS SMASH THE STATE, IT'LL BE UP TO THESE LAWRENCE ANARCHISTS TO SORT THROUGH AND CATALOG THE DEBRIS.

THAT NIGHT, WE STAY AT THE ANARCHIST HOUSE. DEPENDING ON WHO YOU ASK, IT'S EITHER CALLED THE JOE HILL HOUSE OR THE JOHN BROWN HOUSE. MIKE AND I FRY UP SOME TOFU DONATED BY THE LOCAL TOFU FACTORY WHILE JORDAN, ONE OF THE ANARCHIST KIDS, WORKS ON HER PRISON NEWSLETTER. I DAYDREAM ABOUT JOINING JORDAN ON THE BARRICADES, TOSSING MOLOTOV COCKTAILS AND SILKSCREENING T-SHIRTS WITH PITHY SLOGANS. LIVING A LIFE WHERE NO LOST CAUSE ISN'T WORTH FIGHTING FOR.

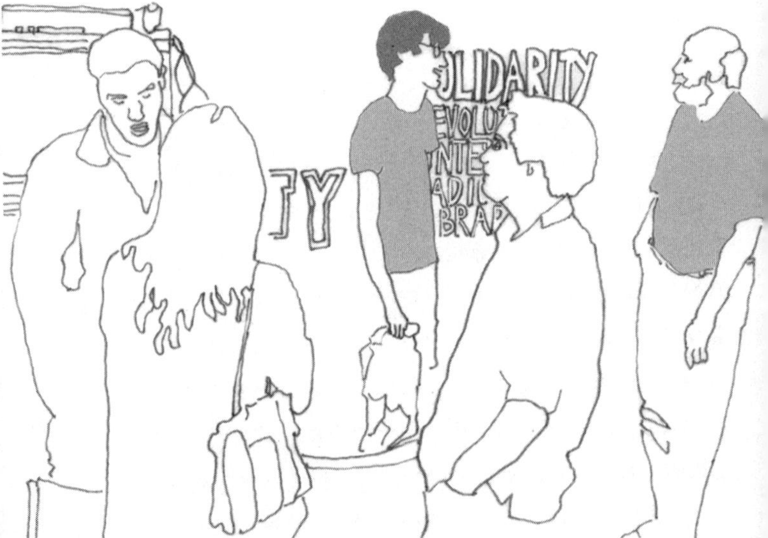

09/19/06

IT'S HARD TO FACE WHAT LIES AHEAD: LONG MILES OF BAD COFFEE AND COLD NIGHTS IN THE TENTS. SO WE STAY IN LAWRENCE ANOTHER DAY. AFTER DARK, WE MEET KHALILA, ANOTHER ONE OF THE ANARCHIST KIDS, AT A COFFEE PLACE DOWNTOWN. AT 11 PM, SHE MAKES AN ANNOUNCEMENT.

"IT'S PIZZA O'CLOCK," SHE SAYS.

A SMALL CROWD OF US TROOP DOWN A NEARBY ALLEY. COLLEGE HIPSTERS, CRUSTY PUNKS, AND A FEW HOMELESS GUYS. WE GATHER AT THE BACK DOOR OF A PIZZA PLACE TILL ONE OF THE WORKERS COMES OUT WITH A COUPLE BOXES OF LEFTOVER SLICES. IT'S SOME KIND OF MAGICAL MOMENT, STANDING IN A DARK ALLEY IN LAWRENCE, KANSAS, HAVING A PIZZA PARTY. THE CRUSTIES HEAR THAT MIKE AND I ARE LEAVING TOWN IN

THE MORNING.

"HOW ABOUT SOME HUGS FOR THE ROAD?" THEY ASK. THEN WE GET BEAR HUGS FROM THE CRUSTIES, WHETHER WE WANT THEM OR NOT.

09/20/06

ON THE WAY OUT OF TOWN, WE DROP BY THE JUICE STOP, THE SMOOTHIE PLACE WHERE JORDAN AND KHALILA WORK. THEY TELL US THAT ONE DAY WHEN THEY GOT REALLY BORED, THEY INVENTED A BUNCH OF VEGAN SMOOTHIES AND NAMED THEM AFTER EARTH CRISIS SONGS: FIRESTORM (BANANAS, RASPBERRIES), ECOCIDE (IT'S GREEN), ETC. THEY HOOK US UP WITH A COUPLE EARTHWORMS: BLUEBERRIES, COCONUT, AND SOY MILK.

EASTERN KANSAS HAS TWO KINDS OF TOPOGRAPHY: THE KIND MADE OUT OF HILLS, AND THE KIND MADE OUT OF WIND. WE SPEND ALL DAY STRUGGLING THROUGH BOTH. BY THE TIME WE GET TO POMONA, LAWRENCE'S FREE PIZZA AND VEGAN SMOOTHIES ARE A FAINT MEMORY. WE GET A BITE AT BUZZARD'S PIZZA, "VOTED #1 IN N.E. KANSAS." VOTED #1 FOR WHAT, I WONDER. WELL-STOCKED NAPKIN DISPENSERS, PERHAPS? CERTAINLY NOT FOR THE PIZZA.

THE DAY IS ALL WIND, HILLS, AND WALMART TRUCKS. WE SPEND THE NIGHT AT A LITTLE STATE PARK. THE RANGER WARNS US THAT RAIN IS ON THE WAY. WE PITCH OUR TENTS AND ATTACH THE RAIN

FLAPS UNDER A SKY THAT IS FOREST FIRE ORANGE.

09/21/06

THE WIND WAKES ME UP, ROARING IN THE TREES AND BUFFETING MY TENT. I FEEL LIKE I'M ADRIFT IN A LIFE RAFT ON A STORMY SEA. MIKE AND I MAKE IT AS FAR AS THE MOTEL JUST UP THE ROAD WHEN THE RAIN STARTS FALLING. IT'S CALLED THE LAMONT HILLS RESORT, THOUGH AS FAR AS I CAN TELL, IT'S JUST A MOM-AND-POP MOTEL WITH A DINER ATTACHED TO IT. WE LINGER ENDLESSLY OVER BREAKFAST, ORDERING FOOD ONE ITEM AT A TIME. COFFEE. OJ. A HOMEMADE CINNAMON BUN. A POACHED EGG. CINNAMON TOAST.

WE'RE HOPING TO WAIT OUT THE RAIN, BUT THE SWEET OLD WAITRESS TELLS US IT'S SUPPOSED TO RAIN ALL DAY. AS BREAKFAST HOURS END AND LUNCH BEGINS, THE WAITRESS TALKS TO THE OWNER AND GETS US A MOTEL ROOM FOR 20 BUCKS. "YOU BOYS DON'T WANT TO BE RIDING IN WEATHER LIKE THIS," SHE TSKS.

MIKE AND I LIE AROUND IN OUR MOTEL ROOM ALL DAY. AROUND 5, THE WEATHER TAKES A TURN FOR THE WORSE. WE SWITCH ON THE TV NEWS. IT REPORTS TORNADOES NEAR CONCORDIA, AND TORNADOES OUTSIDE ABILENE, AND SOMETHING DEFINITELY WORTH KEEPING AN EYE ON NEAR COUNCIL GROVE. THE LOCAL WEATHERMAN STANDS IN FRONT OF A DOPPLER RADAR SCREEN. HE POINTS AT THE BRIGHT

RED THUNDER CELLS LIKE A CORONER POINTING AT THE KNIFE WOUNDS. "DON'T PANIC," HE SAYS, LOOKING PANICKY.

MIKE AND I DECIDE TO GET DINNER, BEFORE IT'S TOO LATE. THE SWEET OLD WAITRESS HAS BEEN REPLACED BY A CUTE FARM GIRL. I ORDER A SLICE OF DUTCH RHUBARB PIE. "FRANK MAKES THE FRUIT PIES," THE WAITRESS SAYS SHYLY. IT'S UNBELIEVABLE, THIS PIE. I ORDER A SECOND SLICE. IT'S POSSIBLE TO ORDER SECONDS, OR EVEN THIRDS, BECAUSE THE PRICES ARE SO LOW. "THIS PLACE," MIKE STAMMERS, "IT'S LIKE BEING IN A TIME WARP." "OR AN EPISODE OF *TWIN PEAKS*," I ADD.

OUTSIDE, IT'S PURE CHAOS. THE WIND ROCKS THE CARS IN THE PARKING LOT AND LASHES THE

RAIN AGAINST THE WINDOW. THE CUTE WAITRESS NOTICES US LOOKING OUTSIDE.

"DON'T BE TOO AFRAID OF THE WEATHER," SHE SMILES, MANAGING IN A SINGLE STROKE TO BREAK MIKE'S HEART AND MY HEART, TOO.

09/22/06

NO MATTER HOW CUTE THE WAITRESSES OR HOW GOOD THE PIE, WE'RE GLAD WHEN THE SUN COMES OUT IN THE MORNING AND WE CAN BE ON OUR WAY.

NOT FAR FROM THE LAMONT HILLS RESORT, MIKE SPOTS A RAIL TRAIL OFF TO THE SIDE OF THE ROAD. WE RIDE IT FOR A WHILE, FOLLOWING THE OLD RAILROAD CORRIDOR THAT THESE LITTLE KANSAS TOWNS ARE STRUNG ALONG LIKE NOT-SO-PRECIOUS GEMS. VASSAR. ADMIRE.

BUSHONG. THE TRAIL IS ROUGH — IT TURNS OUT IT'S STILL IN THE WORKS — SO WE PULL BACK ONTO THE HIGHWAY TO OSAGE CITY. A SEMI HAULING CORN PROMPTLY BLOWS ME OFF THE ROAD. THERE'S A STEEP DROP, SO THE ONLY THING I CAN DO IS HANG ON TIGHT AND TAKE THE PLUNGE. I PLOW THROUGH THIGH-HIGH GRASS TILL I BUMP TO A STOP IN THE BOTTOM OF A DITCH. I SIT THERE FOR A WHILE, SEEING STARS. THEN I HAUL MY BIKE BACK ONTO THE HIGHWAY AND CATCH UP WITH MIKE, WHO HADN'T NOTICED I'D GONE MISSING FOR A WHILE.

"EXPERTS DESIGNED THE TITANIC, GOD DESIGNED THE ARK. WHICH ONE SANK?" READS A CHURCH

MARQUEE IN OSAGE CITY. BURLINGAME IS NEXT, WITH BRICK STREETS SO WIDE THAT PEOPLE PARK IN THE MIDDLE OF THEM. IT'S A HARD GRIND TO THE CAMPGROUND AT LAKE WABAUNSEE. WE'RE RIDING THROUGH THE FLINT HILLS, A PART OF KANSAS THAT KANSANS LIKE TO SUBMIT AS EVIDENCE THAT KANSAS ISN'T AS FLAT AS EVERYONE THINKS.

LAKE WABAUNSEE WAS A PRISONER-OF-WAR CAMP DURING WORLD WAR 2. I TRY TO IMAGINE WHAT IT WAS LIKE FOR THE GERMAN SOLDIERS WHO WERE PLUCKED OUT OF THE BATTLEFIELD AND TRANSPORTED TO REMOTE NORTH KANSAS, LIKE THE WIZARD OF OZ IN REVERSE. I READ THAT THE GERMANS WORKED ON THE LOCAL FARMS AND WERE TREATED PRETTY WELL. IN FACT, ALOT OF

THOSE FARMERS HAD COME FROM GERMANY, TOO, A GENERATION EARLIER. SOME OF THE OLD BARRACKS ARE STILL STANDING. THERE'S A RESTAURANT IN ONE OF THEM, WITH AN ALL-YOU-CAN-EAT SALAD BAR AND A FEW TABLES OF OLD FOLKS WHO WANT TO KNOW WHERE THE HELL WE CAME FROM.

09/23/06

WE STRUGGLE UP ONE HILL AFTER ANOTHER, REWARDED AT THE TOP BY A SWEEPING VIEW AND A THRILL RIDE DOWN THE OTHER SIDE.

"IF YOU COULD RIDE A BIKE ON STORMY SEAS, I BET THIS IS WHAT IT'D BE LIKE," MIKE SAYS.

"MMMRPH!" I SAY.

ON MOST DAYS ALTA VISTA, KANSAS IS PROBABLY A VERY SLEEPY

TOWN. BUT THIS WEEKEND IS "OLD SETTLERS DAYS," AND THE PLACE IS HOPPING. DOWN AT THE CITY PARK, OLD FOLKS ARE SITTING AT CARD TABLES SELLING SHOT GLASSES FEATURING U.S. STATES, AND MATCHBOOKS FROM HOTEL BARS THAT CLOSED DOWN DECADES AGO. I BUY SO MANY BANANA CHOCOLATE CHIP MUFFINS FROM THE LOCAL LUTHERANS THAT I'M INTRODUCED LIKE SOME GLUTTONOUS MUFFIN-EATING DIGNITARY TO THE LITTLE OLD LADY WHO BAKED THEM.

SO THE DAY PASSES LIKE THIS: LISTENING TO FAMILY BANDS PLAYING BLUEGRASS MUSIC UNDER THE PARK SHELTER; AND EATING LUTHERAN BAKED GOODS; AND PLACING BETS WITH MIKE ON WHICH KID WILL WIN THE TODDLERS' FOOT RACE DOWN THE MIDDLE OF MAIN

STREET. AT SOME POINT, THE OLD FOLKS PACK UP THEIR CARD TABLES AND THE CROWD THINS. THEN THE CLOUDS ROLL IN. SUDDENLY, MIKE AND I FIND OURSELVES IN AN EMPTY LITTLE KANSAS TOWN ON A COLD AUTUMN DAY. THAT'S WHEN I DIG THROUGH MY SADDLE BAG AND FROM THE VERY BOTTOM, UNDERNEATH THE EMERGENCY SOCKS AND THE BATHING SUIT I HAVEN'T WORN SINCE OHIOPYLE, PENNSYLVANIA, I PULL OUT MY LONG JOHNS. THE SAME BLUE LONG JOHNS I PEELED OFF IN MAY AND HAVEN'T WORN SINCE. I PUT THEM ON AND SIGH. NOW IT'S CONCLUSIVE. I'M WEARING MY LONG UNDERWEAR. SUMMER IS OVER.

NIGHT FALLS. WE HAVE NO WHERE TO STAY, SO WE PITCH OUR TENTS IN THE CITY PARK. THE SHERIFF'S DEPUTY STOPS BY AND

SHINES HIS FLASHLIGHT AT US. WE TELL HIM WE'RE ON A BIKE TOUR. I CASUALLY MENTION MY GENEROUS SUPPORT OF THE LUTHERAN BAKE SALE. HE LETS US STAY.

09/24/06

IT'S A SUNDAY MORNING AND NOTHING IS OPEN. NO COFFEE. NADA. AS WE GLUMLY PEDAL OUT OF ALTA VISTA, A GUY PULLS OVER AND OFFERS US SOME FROZEN SAUSAGE BISCUITS. WE POLITELY REFUSE. THE GUY KNOWS WE WERE CAMPING IN THE PARK LAST NIGHT. LATER, MIKE AND I FIGURE WE WERE THE BIGGEST CAMPING-IN-THE-PARK NEWS SINCE THE MOTORCYCLE GUY. WE HEARD ABOUT HIM YESTERDAY. HOW HE ROARED

INTO TOWN ONE NIGHT A COUPLE YEARS AGO AND PITCHED A TENT IN THE PARK. SOMEONE CALLED THE SHERIFF'S DEPUTY BECAUSE THE GUY HAD "MOTORCYCLE LOOKS." IN THE MORNING, THE TOWN SENT OUT A DELEGATION TO OFFER HIM COFFEE AND DONUTS. IT'S THIS LAST DETAIL THAT KILLS ME. "HOW COME WE DON'T RANK A DONUT DELEGATION?" I FUME.

WE FOLLOW THE OLD ROCK ISLAND LINE TO DWIGHT. THE SAME RAILROAD THAT LEAD BELLY SANG ABOUT:

"THE ROCK ISLAND LINE IS A
MIGHTY GOOD ROAD,
IF YOU WANT TO RIDE, YOU GOTTA
RIDE IT LIKE YOU FIND IT..."

WHICH I GUESS SHOULD BE OUR THEME SONG.

THE DINER IN DWIGHT IS OPEN — HALLELUJAH — AND WE FIND A TABLE NEXT TO A COUPLE BURLY RAILROAD WORKERS. I ORDER EGGS.

"CAN I GET THOSE POACHED?" I ASK THE WAITRESS.

"YOU NEED CONNECTIONS TO GET YOUR EGGS POACHED HERE," SHE SAYS. SHE'S NOT JOKING. I GET THE EGGS FRIED.

DWIGHT ISN'T A GHOST TOWN, BUT IT HAS PLENTY OF GHOSTLY OLD BUILDINGS ON MAIN STREET, BUILT OUT OF THE SAME BUFF-COLORED LIMESTONE WE SAW IN ALTA VISTA. THERE AREN'T ANY TREES IN THIS PART OF KANSAS, SO THEY BUILT THE BUILDINGS OUT OF ROCK. MOST OF THE ACTIVE BUSINESSES IN DWIGHT ARE NOW IN SOULLESS, STEEL-SIDED SHEDS,

WHILE THESE HANDSOME MASONRY BUILDINGS ARE BOARDED UP.

WE DECIDE TO STOP IN HERINGTON. IT'S A LITTLE ROUGH AROUND THE EDGES, THIS TOWN. LIKE ONE OF THOSE DESERT TOWNS IN ARIZONA OR NEVADA WHERE MOTORCYCLE GANGS GO TO RAISE HELL. AS IT HAPPENS, IT'S ALSO THE PLACE WHERE TERRY NICHOLS, ONE OF THE GUYS BEHIND THE OKLAHOMA CITY BOMBING, BOUGHT A HOUSE BACK IN THE 90'S. HE STASHED BOMB-MAKING SUPPLIES THERE. THIS IS SOMETHING I DOUBT THE LOCAL CHAMBER OF COMMERCE HIGHLIGHTS IN ITS PROMOTIONAL LITERATURE.

MIKE AND I RIDE INTO TOWN AND LOOK FOR A MOTEL. THE FIRST PLACE

WE FIND IS CALLED THE JASMINE STUDIOS AND MOTEL.

"THIS PLACE IS A DUMP," I SAY.

"YEAH," MIKE AGREES.

WE FIND THE OFFICE. AN L.E.D. "OPEN" SIGN BEHIND THE WINDOW WINKS SUGGESTIVELY; THE KIND OF OPEN SIGN THAT MAKES ME THINK THAT WHATEVER IT IS THAT'S OPEN WOULD PROBABLY BE BETTER OFF CLOSED. WE TRY THE DOOR. IT'S LOCKED.

I FORGET THE NAME OF THE NEXT PLACE WE FIND. THE LADY IN THE OFFICE SAYS THEY'RE CLOSED FOR REMODELING. THERE'S NO EVIDENCE OF THIS, UNLESS THE HOLE THAT SOMEONE KICKED THROUGH THE DOOR OF THE OFFICE IS PART OF THE REHAB WORK.

THE MOTEL SITUATION IN TOWN SEEMS HOPELESS, SO WE RIDE BACK TO THE HIGHWAY AND FIND A PLACE THAT LOOKS EXACTLY LIKE A SUPER 8, ONLY IT'S NOT. AS WE'RE CHECKING IN, I NOTICE A PLAQUE ON THE WALL. IT'S A DONOR'S LIST. IT TURNS OUT THAT A GROUP OF LOCAL RESIDENTS POOLED THEIR RESOURCES AND BUILT THEIR VERY OWN MOTEL, A NICE ONE WITH FREE BREAKFAST AND WI-FI. THE LADY AT THE DESK EVEN LETS MIKE AND ME THROW OUR FILTHY CLOTHES IN THE MOTEL'S INDUSTRIAL-SIZED WASHING MACHINE. I GUESS THE SKETCHINESS OF HERINGTON'S MOTELS CAUSED THE TOWN TO BAND TOGETHER TO DO SOMETHING ABOUT IT, THE WAY FOLKS IN FRONTIER DAYS USED TO BAND TOGETHER TO

RAISE A BARN OR RUN OFF A GANG OF OUTLAWS.

09/25/06

HILLS ARE HARD, BUT AT LEAST THERE'S A DOWN FOR EVERY UP. BUT THE WIND IS A HILL YOU'RE NEVER DONE RIDING UP.

"HEY MIKE," I YELL, "THE WIND IS A HILL YOU'RE NEVER DONE RIDING UP!"

MIKE SPITS. MIKE HAS BEEN SPITTING A LOT LATELY. HE SAYS THE WIND IS MESSING WITH HIS HEAD, AND IT MAKES HIM DIZZY. A RAYMOND CHANDLER LINE POPS INTO MY HEAD; SOMETHING ABOUT HOW THE HOT DESERT WINDS IN L.A. – THE SANTA ANAS → MAKE WIVES GRAB THEIR CARVING KNIVES AND STUDY THEIR HUSBANDS'

NECKS. HE COULD HAVE BEEN WRITING ABOUT THIS KANSAS WIND.

WE MAKE IT TO ABILENE. "THE WILDEST TOWN IN THE WEST," IT CLAIMS. THE CHISHOLM TRAIL ENDED HERE. COWBOYS USED TO DRIVE THEIR CATTLE UP THE TRAIL FROM TEXAS. THEN THEY'D LOAD THEM ONTO TRAINS IN ABILENE AND SHIP THEM EAST. THE TOWN USED TO BE ALL SALOONS AND SHOOTOUTS, BUT AS FAR AS MIKE AND I CAN TELL, THINGS HAVE QUIETED DOWN. WHILE WE'RE RUBBERNECKING DOWNTOWN, WE MEET A GUY WHO IS RENOVATING AN OLD BUILDING. HE TELLS US HE'S ORIGINALLY FROM LONGVIEW, TEXAS. HE ALSO TELLS US HE'S A

VIETNAM VET. A SNIPER. 108 CONFIRMED KILLS, AND 39 MORE UNCONFIRMED. HE TELLS US HE WAS ONCE SO WELL CONCEALED IN THE UNDERBRUSH THAT A VIETCONG SOLDIER TOOK A PISS ON HIS LEG AND NEVER NOTICED A THING.

09/26/06

OLD ABILENE IS A FAKE OLD WEST TOWN THAT TAKES UP A SQUARE BLOCK OF PRESENT-ERA ABILENE. IT'S SCHLOCKY AND RUNDOWN; A ROADSIDE ATTRACTION PAST ITS PRIME. DURING THE SUMMER, THERE ARE GUNFIGHTS, AND CAN-CAN GIRLS IN THE ALAMO SALOON. BUT SUMMER IS OVER AND THE WHOLE PLACE IS CLOSED UP TIGHT. IT SEEMS LESS LIKE AN OLD WEST TOWN AND MORE

LIKE AN OLD WEST GHOST TOWN.

A FEW BLOCKS AWAY, THE MUSEUM OF INDEPENDENT TELEPHONY IS OPEN. THE COMPANY THAT ULTIMATELY BECAME SPRINT STARTED IN ABILENE AT THE END OF THE NINETEENTH CENTURY. I'M SURPRISED THAT A MAJOR TELECOM COMPANY STARTED IN A LITTLE TOWN IN KANSAS. BUT ON SECOND THOUGHT, IT MAKES SENSE. ALL THIS LONESOME WIDE OPEN. WHEN YOUR NEAREST NEIGHBOR IS TEN MILES AWAY, A TELEPHONE DEFINITELY COMES IN HANDY.

THE MUSEUM OOZES CORPORATE FUNDING. IT'S GOT A FANCY VIDEO THEATER AND LOTS OF TOUCH-SCREEN DISPLAYS. THE PLACE IS MOSTLY DEDICATED TO A VAST AND VARIED COLLECTION OF VINTAGE

TELEPHONES, FOREIGN AND DOMESTIC, WITH LOTS OF MYSTERIOUS CRANKS AND BUTTONS AND DIALS. A LOT OF THE TELEPHONES ARE CLUNKY, AND REMIND YOU THAT GETTING A HOLD OF SOMEONE FAR AWAY USED TO BE A LOT HARDER. A SLOW STRUGGLE THROUGH SWITCHES AND EXCHANGES; PAST OPERATORS ON THE GRAVEYARD SHIFT; UP AND DOWN THE CATENARY CURVE OF TELEPHONE WIRES STRUNG THROUGH THE DARK. WITH LUCK, YOU COULD CONJURE UP A VOICE ON THE RECEIVER. FAINT AND FAR AWAY. A TRACE. A LITTLE SPARK.

MIKE AND I SPEND THE DAY RIDING TO SALINA. I GOT A CALL FROM LJR A COUPLE DAYS AGO.

"I'M COMING BACK ON THE RIDE," SHE SAID. "WHERE SHOULD WE MEET?"
THERE'S A GREYHOUND STATION IN SALINA, SO WE AGREE TO MEET THERE.

09/27/06

THE BUS STATION IS IN A TRUCK STOP ON THE WEST SIDE OF TOWN. A FEW PEOPLE ARE WAITING FOR THE BUS, WITH THE EXPRESSION YOU WEAR WHEN YOU'RE ABOUT TO TAKE A RIDE ON THE GREYHOUND: A MIXTURE OF RESIGNATION AND DREAD. EVERYONE'S THINKING THE SAME THING: OH GOD, HOW BAD IS IT GOING TO BE THIS TIME?
LJR WALKS OFF THE BUS ALREADY WEARING HER BIKE SHORTS. WE PULL HER BOXED-UP BIKE OUT

FROM UNDER THE BUS AND ASSEMBLE IT IN THE PARKING LOT, UNDER THE THOUGHTFUL GAZE OF BUS PASSENGERS SMOKING CIGARETTES. A GUY PULLS UP IN A MINIVAN AND ASKS US ABOUT OUR TRIP. HE TELLS US HE'S ALWAYS WANTED TO GO ON A LONG BIKE TRIP BUT HE'S NEVER HAD THE NERVE. THEN HE APOLOGIZES FOR HIS MINIVAN. "IT'S MY WIFE'S," HE EXPLAINS, WHICH I GUESS IS HIS SHORTHAND WAY OF APOLOGIZING FOR HIS WHOLE LIFE, AND ALL ITS COMPROMISES AND SMALL DEFEATS. WHEN HE DRIVES AWAY, LJR AND I DECIDE HE WAS A PHANTOM: THE GHOST OF THINGS REGRETTED. LJR WANTS TO BURN SOME SAGE OR PERFORM A PURIFICATION RITUAL. BECAUSE THAT'S A GHOST YOU NEVER WANT TO GET A VISIT FROM.

09/28/06

NOW THERE'S THREE OF US AGAIN AND EVERYONE WE MEET IS FRIENDLY. IS IT BECAUSE THREE CYCLISTS SEEM LESS THREATENING THAN TWO? MORE LIKELY, IT'S BECAUSE ONE OF THE CYCLISTS IS LJR. SHE'S LIKE AN ENERGY VORTEX. A PLACE WHERE THE MYSTERIOUS FORCES OF THE COSMOS COLLECT. NOW THAT SHE'S BACK, EVERYONE WANTS TO KNOW WHERE WE'RE COMING FROM AND WHERE WE'RE HEADED. AT THIS POINT, THE ANSWER ISN'T SO EASY: I'M FROM TEXAS, BUT I'M RIDING FROM D.C.; MIKE IS FROM PHILLY BUT HE'S BEEN RIDING SINCE ST. LOUIS; AND LJR IS FROM CHICAGO AND STARTED RIDING IN D.C., BUT THEN STOPPED IN MANSFIELD, OHIO AND

WENT BACK TO CHICAGO, THEN JOINED THE RIDE AGAIN IN SALINA, KANSAS; AND ALL OF US ARE HEADED TO DENVER. MAYBE.
OF COURSE, NO ONE ACTUALLY WANTS to HEAR ALL THIS. SO SOMETIMES WE TELL PEOPLE WE'RE COMING FROM THE LAST TOWN WE WERE IN, AND WE'RE HEADING FOR THE NEXT TOWN UP THE ROAD. AND SOMETIMES, WE JUST STAND THERE SMILING LIKE IDIOTS.

09/29/06

IN THE MORNING, WE FIND A NOTE TAPED TO THE DOOR OF OUR MOTEL ROOM. ON THE FRONT IS A CLIP ART PICTURE OF A COFFEE CUP. ON THE BACK, IT SAYS "CONTINENTAL BREAKFAST IS AVAILABLE IN THE ICE ROOM." THE ICE ROOM IS A FEW STEPS AWAY, BEHIND A DOOR

WITH ANOTHER NOTE TAPED TO IT. "ICE ROOM," THE NOTE SAYS. MOST OF THE ICE ROOM IS TAKEN UP BY A BIG OLD ICE MACHINE. THERE ARE ALSO SHELVES STACKED WITH CLEANING SUPPLIES AND TOWELS. IT TAKES A FEW MINUTES TO TRACK DOWN THE CONTINENTAL BREAKFAST. THE COFFEE POT IS ON TOP OF THE ICE MACHINE. THERE'S A CARTON OF ORANGE JUICE IN A STYROFOAM BEER COOLER ON THE FLOOR NEXT TO AN OLD TIRE. THREE INDIVIDUALLY WRAPPED DONUTS SIT ON TOP OF THREE INDIVIDUALLY WRAPPED ROLLS OF TOILET PAPER.

IT'S A HILLY RIDE TO LUCAS, BUT WE'RE TOO EXCITED TO CARE. LUCAS IS THE FOLK ART CAPITAL OF KANSAS. MOST PEOPLE KNOW ABOUT LUCAS BECAUSE OF THE

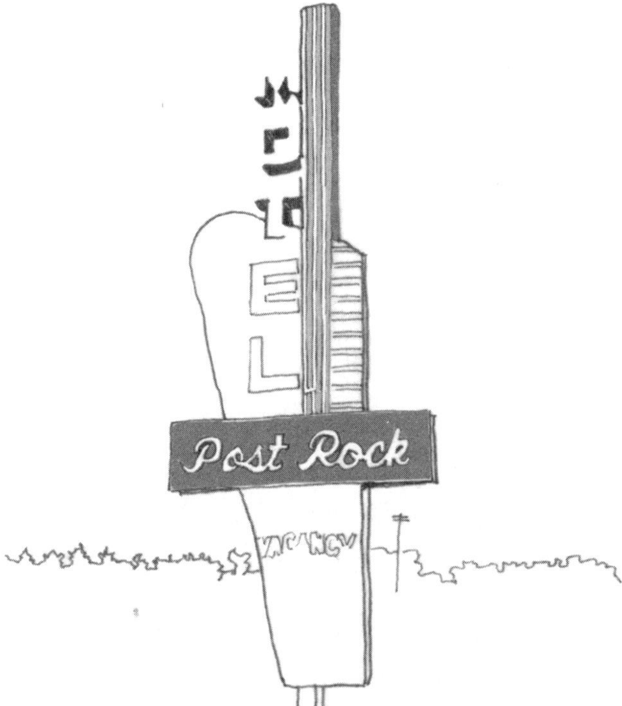
Post Rock

GARDEN OF EDEN. IT WAS BUILT IN THE EARLY 1900'S BY A LOCAL GUY NAMED SAMUEL DINSMOOR, A FARMER AND CIVIL WAR VET WHO TURNED HIS HOUSE INTO A SHRINE TO AMERICAN DEMOCRACY AND TEDDY ROOSEVELT-STYLE PROGRESSIVISM. MUCH TO HIS NEIGHBORS' CONFUSION AND DISMAY, HE ERECTED GIANT CONCRETE TREES IN HIS YARD AND SUSPENDED CREEPY CONCRETE FIGURES FROM THEM. EVERYTHING IS ALLEGORICAL. A MONOPOLIST OCTOPUS WITH LONG, LOOPING TENTACLES STRANGLES FARMERS AND SHOPKEEPERS. AVENGING ANGELS SMITE BANKERS AND OLIGARCHS WITH FIERY SWORDS. IT'S OCCUPY WALL STREET, A CENTURY BEFORE AND 1500 MILES WEST OF WALL STREET. DINSMOOR IS STILL THERE, STASHED

AWAY LIKE A NEW WORLD PHARAOH IN A LIMESTONE PYRAMID HE BUILT IN HIS BACKYARD.

THERE WAS ANOTHER FOLK ARTIST IN TOWN, A LITTLE OLD LADY NAMED FLORENCE DEEBLE. BACK IN THE 1950'S, SHE USED CEMENT TO RECREATE POSTCARD PICTURES OF FAMOUS TOURIST DESTIN-ATIONS LIKE MT. RUSHMORE AND THE FOUR CORNERS MONUMENT IN HER BACK YARD. LITTLE MONUMENTS TO PLACES SHE ONCE VISITED OR ALWAYS DREAMED OF VISITING. A PRIVATE SCULPTURE PARK OF HER HEART'S DESIRES.

"WHAT IS IT ABOUT THIS TOWN?" I ASK THE LADY AT THE DOWNTOWN ART CENTER. SHE SMILES AND SHRUGS. I GUESS IT'S HARD TO PUT

YOUR FINGER ON IT. THAT NAMELESS THING THAT RISES UP FROM SOME FISSURE IN THE LIMESTONE, AND GETS CAUGHT IN THE WIND, AND DRIFTS THROUGH WINDOW SCREENS ON WARM SUMMER NIGHTS. SOMETHING FROM BEFORE THE SOD WAS BROKEN THAT CAN DRIVE A MILD-MANNERED KANSAN A LITTLE CRAZY.

WE GET DINNER AT A DINER ON MAIN STREET. IT'S A LOCAL CROWD: OLD WHEAT FARMERS; SOME FAMILIES. WE RUN INTO ERIC ABRAHAM, A SWEET OLD SCULPTOR AND SELF-DESCRIBED "PROFESSIONAL PROFESSOR OF PORCELAIN PROFICIENCY," WHO WE MET EARLIER. HE INTRODUCES US TO HIS FRIEND, PILAR, A MIDDLE AGED LADY WHO TELLS US SHE'S AN

ALIEN FROM THE SIRIAN STAR SYSTEM. EVEN THOUGH PILAR TALKS LOUDLY ABOUT THE DAY SHE DISCOVERED "THE BEAUTY OF THE LINE," AND EVEN THOUGH ERIC SWEARS LIKE A SAILOR, NO ONE IN THE PLACE GIVES US A DIRTY LOOK. I GUESS THEY'RE USED TO IT. "THE LUCAS TRIANGLE," THAT'S HOW THE LOCALS DESCRIBE THEIR TOWN.

09/30/06

SEPTEMBER IS ALMOST OVER, WHICH MEANS TWO MONTHS ON THE ROAD. I VAGUELY RECALL SOME OTHER LIFE BEFORE THE BIKE RIDE, BUT THE MEMORY OF IT FADES A LITTLE MORE EACH DAY.

AFTER BREAKFAST, WE STROLL DOWN MAIN STREET, FAT-BELLIED AND COFFEED-UP, TOOTHPICKS HANGING FROM OUR LIPS. THEN WE SPOT IT:

A SMALL SCHOOL BUS PAINTED WITH FAT RED AND WHITE STRIPES. "THE WORLD'S LARGEST COLLECTION OF THE WORLD'S SMALLEST VERSIONS OF THE WORLD'S LARGEST THINGS," READS A SIGN PAINTED ACROSS THE SIDE OF THE BUS.

THE CREATOR OF THE COLLECTION, ERIKA, INVITES US IN. LUCAS HAS BEEN HER HOMEBASE FOR YEARS, BUT SHE'S USUALLY ON THE ROAD, TRAVELING FROM ONE 'WORLD'S LARGEST' THING TO ANOTHER — THE WORLD'S LARGEST BALL OF TWINE IN DARWIN, MINNESOTA, FOR INSTANCE, OR THE WORLD'S LARGEST PAPER CUP IN RIVERSIDE, CALIFORNIA. THEN SHE MAKES A MINIATURE VERSION OF THE LARGEST THING AND MOUNTS IT IN HER BUS, WHICH IS A MOBILE GALLERY OF THE SMALLEST LARGEST STUFF. THE BUS IS PRETTY PLUSH.

THERE'S A COMFY BED AND A BIG TABLE STACKED WITH MAPS AND GUIDE BOOKS. MINIATURE LARGEST THINGS ARE TUCKED IN EVERY NOOK AND CRANNY: THE WORLD'S LARGEST BOX OF RAISINS, THE WORLD'S LARGEST 8-BALL, THE WORLD'S LARGEST TALKING PAUL BUNYAN. MY HEART SOMEHOW MANAGES TO LEAP AND SINK AT THE EXACT SAME TIME. BECAUSE HERE IT IS, THE PERFECT ART PROJECT, MAYBE EVEN THE PERFECT LIFE, BUT IT ALREADY BELONGS TO SOMEONE ELSE.

WHEN WE FINALLY ROLL OUT OF THE LUCAS TRIANGLE, THE SUN IS SHINING AND THE AIR IS STILL. IT'S THE FIRST REALLY GOOD BIKE RIDING DAY SINCE WE'VE BEEN IN KANSAS. IN NO TIME, WE'RE IN LURAY AND DUCK INTO CAFÉ LURAY FOR EGG

SALAD SANDWICHES. THE CAFE HAS A FOR SALE SIGN TAPED TO THE WINDOW. WE'VE BEEN NOTICING A LOT OF FOR SALE SIGNS LATELY.

"IT'S LIKE WE'RE SEEING THE END OF SOMETHING," LJR SAYS.

IT'S GETTING DARK AS WE RIDE INTO SMITH CENTER, HOMETOWN OF FATTY ARBUCKLE. WE'RE WAY UP NORTH NOW, JUST SHY OF THE NEBRASKA STATE LINE. THE PEOPLE WE MEET AREN'T UNFRIENDLY, BUT THEY'RE DEFINITELY NO-NONSENSE AND A LITTLE RESERVED. MAYBE IT'S BECAUSE IT DOESN'T RAIN MUCH UP HERE, AND THE LAND'S NOT SO FERTILE. IN A PLACE LIKE THAT, YOU DON'T WASTE ANYTHING, INCLUDING YOUR BREATH. ALL THE SWEETNESS THAT PEOPLE AROUND HERE DON'T EXPRESS IS BAKED INTO THEIR PIES.

BIG-HEARTED, GENEROUS PIES. DUTCH-APPLE, STRAWBERRY-RHUBARB, AND COCONUT CREAM. RICH, CREAMY, OVERSEXED PIES THAT PRACTICALLY OOZE OFF THE PLATE AND PLOP ON YOUR LAP.

ON THE WAY TO THE CAMPGROUND, LJR INSISTS WE STOP AT A PLACE CALLED PAUL'S CAFE. SHE HAS A GOOD FEELING ABOUT THE PIE. THE PLACE JUST CLOSED, BUT LJR MANAGES TO GET A FEW SLICES OF BANANA CREAM IN PIE-WEDGE-SHAPED TAKE-OUT BOXES. NEXT DOOR TO THE CAFE IS THE U.S. CENTER MOTEL, NAMED FOR THE FACT THAT BOTH THE GEOGRAPHIC AND GEODETIC CENTERS OF THE CONTINENTAL UNITED STATES ARE LOCATED AROUND HERE SOMEWHERE. THE MOTEL HAS A BIG NEON SIGN OUT FRONT. THE WORD 'MOTEL' GLOWS HOT PINK. WE DECIDE TO HAVE A

LOOK. THE OWNER IS A GUY FROM THE PHILIPPINES. HE RUNS THE PLACE WITH HIS TWO TEEN-AGED NIECES WHO RECENTLY IMMIGRATED TO KANSAS. WE CHAT WITH THEM FOR A WHILE AND I GET A LITTLE CHOKED UP. I MEAN, HERE WE ARE AT THE CENTER OF THE U.S., AT THE U.S. CENTER MOTEL, AND IT'S RUN BY RECENT IMMIGRANTS LOOKING FOR A BETTER LIFE. ONE OF THE TWO NIECES HANDS ME A KEY TO THE ROOM.

"HERE WE ARE IN THE MIDDLE OF AMERICA," SHE SAYS, ROLLING HER EYES. "HORRAY."

10/01/06

I'M UP EARLY, SO I LEAF THROUGH A PROMOTIONAL PAMPHLET PUBLISHED BY THE SMITH CENTER CHAMBER OF COMMERCE. "OUR CENTERED LOCATION JUST 14 MILES FROM THE GEOGRAPHIC

CENTER OF THE 48 CONTIGUOUS STATES— HAS ALLOWED US TO DEVELOP A LIFESTYLE OF TRADITIONAL AMERICAN VALUES," IT SAYS. I READ THIS STATEMENT A COUPLE TIMES, BUT I'M NOT SURE I KNOW WHAT IT MEANS. IS THE SMITH CENTER CHAMBER OF COMMERCE SAYING THERE IS A ZERO POINT OR GROUND ZERO OF TRADITIONAL AMERICAN VALUES LOCATED IN A WHEAT FIELD 14 MILES OUTSIDE OF TOWN — A SITE OF UNIMAGINABLE AMERICAN VALUES-NESS? AND IF SO, DO THOSE VALUES RADIATE OUTWARD LIKE RADIO WAVES, LOSING INTENSITY AS THEY TRAVEL FARTHER AND FARTHER FROM THE SOURCE? THIS WOULD HAVE SOBERING IMPLICATIONS FOR CERTAIN FARAWAY STATES — SOUTH CAROLINA, FOR INSTANCE, 1200 MILES TO THE SOUTHEAST — THAT

THOUGHT THEY HAD A LOCK ON THE WHOLE TRADITIONAL AMERICAN VALUES THING.

WHILE I'M WAITING FOR LJR AND MIKE TO WAKE UP, I MEET GILLIAN. HE'S A CYCLIST FROM L.A. WHO IS RIDING EAST TO MISSOURI TO MEET HIS WIFE AND BIKE THE KATY TRAIL. HE ASKS TO BORROW SOME TIRE PATCHES. HE TELLS ME HE WENT THROUGH A WHOLE BOX IN WESTERN KANSAS, THANKS TO THE GOAT HEAD THISTLES.

"WHAT ARE GOAT HEAD THISTLES?" I ASK. GILLIAN'S EYES SPARK.

"THEY'RE MISERABLE LITTLE BASTARDS THAT'LL POKE A HOLE THROUGH ANY TIRE OUT THERE. WHATEVER YOU DO, KEEP YOUR BIKE

OFF THE GRASS."

IN SMITH CENTER, WE PICK UP HIGHWAY 36. AFTER 1500 MILES OF ZIGGING AND ZAGGING; BACK ROADS AND DETOURS AND ALTERNATE ROUTES; AFTER TWO MONTHS OF MISSED TURNS, DEAD ENDS AND BRIDGES OUT, WE ARRIVE AT THE HIGHWAY THAT WILL TAKE US STRAIGHT ACROSS NORTHERN KANSAS AND ALL THE WAY TO DENVER. FROM NOW ON, WE DON'T NEED MAPS OR CUE SHEETS. IT'S ALL HIGHWAY 36.

ON THE WAY TO LIVINGSTON, THE WIND HITS. A SINGLE-MINDED WIND FROM THE SOUTH THAT MUST BE ON ITS WAY TO SOME PLACE PRETTY DAMN IMPORTANT, BECAUSE IT PLOWS RIGHT INTO US WITH NO APOLOGIES. AT SOME POINT, I GET T-BONED BY A BIG TUMBLEWEED THAT ROLLS OUT OF NO WHERE AND GETS JAMMED BETWEEN

MY LEGS. MIKE SEES THE WHOLE THING HAPPEN. HE THINKS IT'S HILARIOUS. THINKING BACK, THIS IS PROBABLY WHEN MIKE'S BIKE KARMA WENT BAD. LITTLE DOES HE KNOW THE GOAT HEAD TORMENT THAT AWAITS HIM.

OUTSIDE PHILIPSBURG, I GET MY FOURTH FLAT OF THE BIKE TRIP. A RUSTY METAL STAPLE DOES THE HIT. AS I'M FIXING THE FRONT TIRE, I NOTICE THAT MY REAR TIRE IS NEARLY BALD. I BOUGHT THAT TIRE NEW BEFORE I GOT TO D.C. IT HAD A BEEFY TREAD THAT'S NOW BEEN WORN CLEAN AWAY BY THE SLOW, STEADY WEAR OF THE MILES. THAT REAR TIRE MAKES ME FEEL PROUD. LIKE I'VE REALLY GONE SOMEWHERE.

AT THE GROCERY STORE IN PHILIPSBURG, A YOUNG GUY CHATS WITH US. HE

LOOKS KIND OF RUMPLED. LIKE MAYBE HE'S LIVING OUT OF HIS CAR. "WHERE YA STAYING TONIGHT?" HE ASKS. WE TELL HIM WE DON'T KNOW. THE GUY POINTS AT A CHURCH ACROSS THE STREET. "ASK REVEREND MARK. HE LIKES BIKES."

WE NOMINATE LJR TO KNOCK ON THE DOOR OF THE RECTORY. REV. MARK'S WIFE ANSWERS, HOLDING A BABY. SHE TELLS US MARK IS VISITING THE HOSPITAL, BUT OF COURSE IT'D BE OKAY TO CAMP ON THE LITTLE LAWN NEXT TO THE CHURCH.

WE PITCH OUR TENTS IN THE SHADOWS. THEN WE MAKE SOME PRETTY MEAN AVOCADO SANDWICHES AND CHOW DOWN ON THE CHURCH STEPS. THE LOCAL COP DRIVES BY, GOOD AND SLOW. BUT SOMEHOW, THE SIGHT OF

THREE SCRUFFY STRANGERS EATING SANDWICHES ON THE STEPS OF THE PRESBYTERIAN CHURCH DOESN'T WARRANT FURTHER INVESTIGATION, AND HE DRIVES AWAY.

REV. MARK SHOWS UP AN HOUR LATER. HE'S A GUY IN HIS 30'S WHO MOVED OUT TO KANSAS FROM PITTSBURG, PA.

"I ASKED GOD WHERE I SHOULD GO, AND GOD TOLD ME TO GO TO PHILIPSBURG, KANSAS," MARK SAYS WITH A SMIRK. LIKE MAYBE GOD IS KIND OF A DICK. OR A JOKESTER. A CRAZY UNCLE MURRAY OF A GOD WHO'S ALWAYS PLAYING PRACTICAL JOKES ON US.

IT TURNS OUT REV. MARK IS A CYCLIST. HE TELLS US ABOUT HIS FAVORITE RIDE, THE STARBUCKS CENTURY, A HUNDRED MILE LOOP

TO THE NEAREST STARBUCKS.

AFTER MARK SAYS GOODNIGHT, I LIE AWAKE IN MY TENT FOR A WHILE. MAYBE IT'S BECAUSE I'M CAMPING ON A CHURCH LAWN, BUT I THINK ABOUT GOD SOME MORE. I'M NOT SURE GOD TALKS TO US, BUT SOMETIMES I THINK HE MIGHT BE AROUND, STANDING IN THE SHADOWS, STARING UP AT OUR BEDROOM WINDOW WHILE WE SLEEP. JUST STANDING THERE, QUIET.

10/02/06

IN THE MORNING, REV. MARK BRINGS US SOME COFFEE. "IT'S PART SOMETHING FANCY, AND PART WALMART FRENCH ROAST," HE TELLS US. I'VE BEEN READING JACK LONDON'S STORIES ABOUT THE TIME HE SPENT AS A HOBO. LONDON

WOULD CALL THIS COFFEE "FIREMEN'S JAVA," BECAUSE THE GUYS ON THE STEAM ENGINES WHO SHOVELED COAL – FIREMEN – MADE THE BEST COFFEE.

WE ROLL INTO TOWN AND GET BREAKFAST AT 3RD STREET BAKERY. LJR ORDERS HER EGGS BRAISED. "WHAT'S BRAISED?" I ASK. "IT'S WHEN THEY FRY AN EGG, THEN POUR WATER ON IT AND PUT A LID OVER IT," LJR EXPLAINS. I GET A CINNAMON BUN THAT'S MADE SMALL-TOWN-KANSAS STYLE, WHICH IS TO SAY, NO HOLDS BARRED. IT'S WAY TOO BIG AND OOZING SUGAR AND WHOLE PECANS. THE OLD FOLKS AT THE OLD FOLKS' TABLE ASK WHERE YA FROM?. WHERE YA HEADED?. LJR AND MIKE

LOOK AT ME. AT FIRST, IT WAS FUN TO ANSWER THESE QUESTIONS, BUT NOT ANYMORE. IT'S JUST THAT THE RESPONSES WE GET ARE UNPREDICTABLE. SOMETIMES PEOPLE ARE EXCITED TO HEAR ABOUT ALL THE MILES WE'VE BIKED. BUT OTHER TIMES THEY GET A LOOK IN THEIR EYE. MAYBE BECAUSE THEY FEEL STUCK IN A LIFE THAT DOESN'T ALLOW FOR A BIG BIKE RIDE. OR MAYBE BECAUSE THEY WONDER WHAT KIND OF SELF-RESPECTING PERSON WOULD GO ON A BIKE RIDE LIKE THAT.

WE LEAVE PHILLIPSBURG AND PASS THROUGH STUTTGART. THE TOWN WAS FOUNDED BY GERMANS WHO PRONOUNCED THE NAME "SH-TOOT-GAHRT." BUT NOW THE CHILDREN OF THE CHILDREN OF THE CHILDREN

OF THOSE GERMAN SETTLERS PRONOUNCE IT "STUTT-GART." I GUESS IT'S ALWAYS LIKE THAT. EVERYTHING GOES NATIVE. AND WHEN IT DOESN'T, IT'S OUT OF PLACE. THE LONELINESS OF THE EXOTIC SPECIES.

WE TAKE A BREAK IN PRAIRIE VIEW, POPULATION 116. ANOTHER OLD WHISTLE STOP ALONG THE ROCK ISLAND LINE. WE FIND A LITTLE PARK. MIKE STARTS TO ROLL HIS BIKE ONTO THE GRASS.

"UH, MIKE–" I SAY, BUT IT'S TOO LATE. A GOAT HEAD LUNGES. IN SECONDS, IT'S OVER. MIKE'S REAR TIRE SHRIVELS.

"BUT ALL I DID WAS ROLL INTO THE GRASS!" MIKE SPUTTERS. MIKE COMES FROM PHILLY, WHERE GRASS IS SOMETHING TO LAZE ON. WELCOME TO KANSAS, MIKE.

WE GET TO THE NATURAL FOOD STORE IN NORTON JUST AS IT'S CLOSING. WE PLEAD OUR CASE WITH JIM, THE OWNER: WE'RE VEGETARIANS ADRIFT IN THE CARNIVOROUS WASTES OF KANSAS! PLEASE! JIM HAS PITY ON US AND HEATS UP SOME LEFTOVERS: VEGGIE LASAGNA, GREEK PIZZA, AND GREEN SALAD ON THE SIDE. IT'S THE BEST MEAL SINCE LAWRENCE.

JIM'S STORE IS CALLED 'PURE PRAIRIE.' JIM IS ALL ABOUT PURITY. HE TELLS US THAT PURE FOOD FEEDS A PURE SPIRIT. HE'S AN ORGANIC FARMER AND A CHRISTIAN. NOT SOME NAMBY-PAMBY MAINSTREAM CHRISTIAN, EITHER, BUT A FIERY CHRISTIAN SOLDIER WHO BELIEVES IN A WRATHFUL GOD. WHEN JIM

TALKS, HIS EYEBROWS STAY FIXED, AND HIS EYES SHOOT YOU WITH BRIGHT BLUE LASER BEAMS. AND WHEN HE SAYS MONSANTO'S GENETICALLY MODIFIED SEEDS ARE SATANIC, HE'S DEFINITELY NOT SPEAKING FIGURATIVELY. JIM'S GOD SEEMS LIKE THE KIND OF DEITY THAT MIGHT TURN A BLIND EYE IF SOMEONE WERE TO, SAY, TORCH A TRUCK FULL OF G.M.O. ACORN SQUASH.

10/03/06

IN THE MORNING, WE'RE BACK AT PURE PRAIRIE. JIM MAKES US BREAKFAST — ORGANIC EGGS, ORGANIC OATMEAL, FAIR TRADE COFFEE — WHILE EXPLAINING HOW CORPORATE AGRICULTURE IS ENGAGED IN A SATANIC CONSPIRACY TO

CONTROL THE WORLD'S FOOD SUPPLY.
"YOU KNOW, I KIND OF AGREE WITH THAT DUDE," MIKE SAYS AFTER WE LEAVE.
"ME TOO," LJR SAYS.
"ME TOO," I SAY.

WE MAKE ONE LAST STOP BEFORE WE LEAVE NORTON: THE GALLERY OF THE ALSO-RANS. IT'S A PORTRAIT GALLERY OF EVERY U.S. PRESIDENTIAL CANDIDATE WHO LOST. THE GALLERY IS ON THE SECOND FLOOR OF THE FIRST STATE BANK. A FIDGETY LADY IN A PANT SUIT GREETS US. SHE TELLS US THAT IN ADDITION TO HER DUTIES AS A SECRETARY AT THE BANK, SHE GIVES GUIDED TOURS OF THE GALLERY. THEN SHE LAUNCHES IN TO HER SPIEL.
"THESE MEN BUILT THIS COUNTRY

AND I APPLAUD THEM," SHE SAYS, MOTIONING TOWARD A WALL HUNG WITH THE PORTRAITS OF LOSING CANDIDATES FROM THE 18TH AND 19TH CENTURIES. THEN SHE LOWERS HER VOICE. "BUT THOSE LAST FOUR AROUND THE CORNER,"—GEORGE BUSH, SR., BOB DOLE, AL GORE, AND JOHN KERREY—"I THINK THEY'RE PULLING OUR COUNTRY APART." TWO THINGS STRIKE ME ABOUT THIS LADY'S COMMENTS. FIRST, I'M NOT SURE HOW MUCH I WANT TO APPLAUD THE POLITICIANS OF THE 18TH AND 19TH CENTURIES, WHO INCLUDE A GOOD NUMBER OF SLAVE HOLDERS, INDIAN KILLERS, AND CORPORATE STOOGES. AND SECOND, DOES SHE REALLY BELIEVE THAT KANSAS' OWN FAVORITE SON, BOB DOLE, IS TEARING OUR COUNTRY APART?

THE LADY SLOWLY GUIDES US FROM ONE PICTURE TO THE NEXT, OCCASIONALLY READING HIGHLIGHTS FROM THE INDEX CARDS HUNG NEXT TO THE CANDIDATES. I LINGER FOR A WHILE IN FRONT OF THE PICTURE OF DARLINGTON HOOPES, THE SOCIALIST PARTY CANDIDATE WHO RAN AGAINST EISENHOWER IN '52 AND, AGAIN, IN '56. I'VE NEVER EVEN HEARD OF DARLINGTON HOOPES, BUT I'M GLAD HE'S MEMORIALIZED SOMEWHERE.

THE GALLERY WAS STARTED BACK IN THE 1960'S BY THE BANK'S FORMER PRESIDENT, W.W. ROUSE. I GOOGLE HIM UP LATER, BUT ASIDE FROM REFERENCES TO THE GALLERY, THE ONLY MENTION OF HIM I FIND IS IN THE JULY, 1952 ISSUE OF THE ROTARIAN MAGAZINE.

THERE WAS A CONTEST TO WRITE THE LAST LINE OF THIS LIMERICK:

"THERE WAS A SLICK FELLOW
NAMED MORROW,
WHO ALWAYS WANTED TO BORROW.
BUT IF YOU "TOUCHED" HIM,
YOUR CHANCES WERE SLIM,

W.W. ROUSE'S ENTRY WAS SELECTED AS ONE OF THE TEN BEST:

"AND IF HE "TOUCHED" YOU,
YOU WOULD SORROW."

THE WIND IS BLOWING FROM THE NORTH AS WE LEAVE NORTON, AND IT GETS STRONGER AS THE DAY GOES ON; LEANING INTO US LIKE SOME DRUNK BUDDY YOU'RE WALKING HOME FROM A BAR. WE TAKE A BREAK IN NORCATUR. A PEELING BILLBOARD ALONG THE HIGHWAY IDENTIFIES NORCATUR AS 'THE HOME

OF ELDEN AUKER.' IT TURNS OUT AUKER WAS A MAJOR LEAGUE BASEBALL PLAYER BACK IN THE 1930'S, BUT WE DON'T KNOW THIS AT THE TIME, AND WE DON'T KNOW THAT HE JUST DIED A COUPLE MONTHS EARLIER DOWN IN FLORIDA. ALL WE KNOW IS THAT NORCATUR, KANSAS LOOKS LIKE A TOWN THAT COULD USE A VISIT FROM ITS FAVORITE SON. THE POST OFFICE IS STILL OPEN. I GO INSIDE AND BUY A PRE-STAMPED ENVELOPE. "THANKS FOR THE SALE!" THE POSTAL CLERK SAYS ENTHUSIASTICALLY.

LJR TAKES THE LEAD AND PUSHES US HARD THROUGH HILLS AND HEADWINDS INTO OBERLIN. "LAST INDIAN RAID IN THE STATE OF KANSAS," SAYS A SIGN AT THE

CITY LIMITS. "WHERE FRIENDS MEET ON THE COBBLED STREETS," SAYS ANOTHER. WE GET DINNER AT A BAR CALLED THE RE-LOAD, THEN GO LOOKING FOR A PLACE TO SLEEP. AS WE WALK PAST THE MASONIC HALL, A BIG MASON WITH A BIG BUSHY BEARD WALKS OUT AND SAYS HELLO. HE USED TO BE THE SCOUTMASTER OF THE LOCAL BOY SCOUT TROOP, BUT LIKE A LOT OF OTHER STUFF IN NORTHERN KANSAS, THE SCOUT TROOP HAS FADED AWAY. THE GUY TELLS US THE SCOUTS USED TO MEET IN AN OLD CHURCH HE OWNS, AND HE OFFERS TO LET US CAMP THERE FOR THE NIGHT.

THE CHURCH IS ON A SLEEPY RESIDENTIAL STREET. IT TAKES THE SCOUTMASTER A WHILE TO OPEN THE DOOR.

"HAVEN'T BEEN HERE SINCE THE

TROOP DISBANDED," HE TELLS US. "THE GIRL SCOUTS STILL USE THE PLACE, THOUGH."

THE CHURCH IS A BIG, DRAFTY SPACE WITH A STAGE UP FRONT. NO PEWS. A HAND-LETTERED SIGN TAPED TO THE WALL LISTS "THE GIRL SCOUT LAW" — I WILL DO MY BEST TO BE HONEST, FAIR, CHEERFUL, ETC.

"WHY CHEERFUL?" LJR ASKS. "WHY NOT 'DANGEROUS?' WHY NOT 'BAD-ASS?'"

LJR SLEEPS ON THE STAGE, WHILE MIKE AND I STRETCH OUT ON THE WOODEN FLOOR. IT'S A WINDY NIGHT. I KEEP WAKING UP TO THE SOUND OF THINGS KNOCKING ON THE WALLS AND SKITTERING ACROSS THE ROOF. THE RESTLESS GHOSTS OF BEREFT BOY SCOUTS.

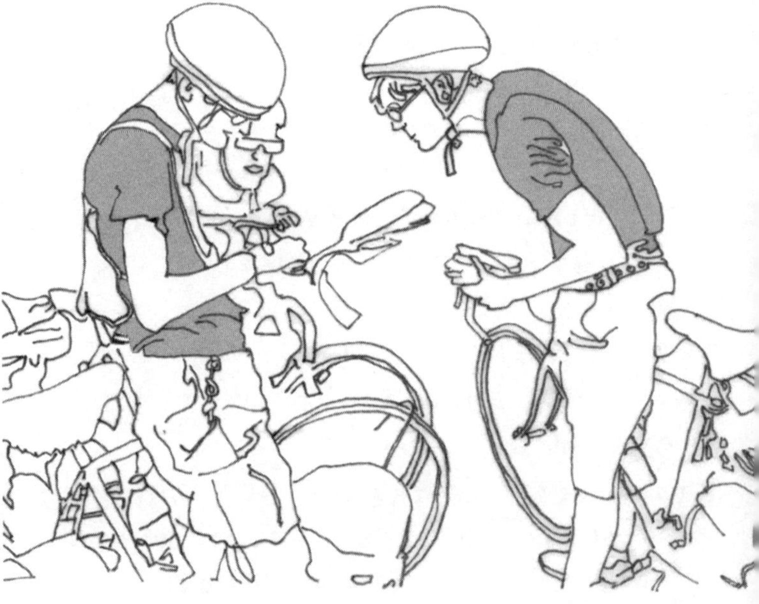

10/04/06

CLEAR AND COLD THIS MORNING. I'VE STARTED TO WEAR A SKI HAT UNDER MY HELMET AND GLOVES ON MY HANDS. WE'VE RIDDEN OUT OF ONE SEASON AND INTO THE NEXT.

BREAKFAST AT THE FRONTIER MOTEL: PEANUT BUTTER CINNAMON BUNS, POACHED EGGS, AND THE FIRST SALSA IN NEARLY 2000 MILES. NOT KETCHUP OR TABASCO. SALSA. INDISPUTABLE EVIDENCE THAT WE'VE CROSSED SOME INVISIBLE BORDER FROM THE MIDWEST TO THE WEST. FROM HERE ON, FARMS WILL GIVE WAY TO CATTLE RANCHES, AND GUYS WEARING BASEBALL HATS WITH SEED COMPANY LOGOS WILL BE REPLACED BY GUYS WEARING COWBOY HATS.

WE RIDE TO ATWOOD, ANOTHER COUNTY

SEAT IN THE CHAIN OF COUNTY SEATS THAT ARE SPACED OUT EVERY 30 MILES OR SO ALONG HIGHWAY 36: OBERLIN (DECATUR COUNTY); ATWOOD (RAWLINS COUNTY); ST. FRANCIS (CHEYENNE COUNTY). SOMEONE TELLS US 30 MILES WAS THE DISTANCE A PONY EXPRESS RIDER COULD RIDE BEFORE CHANGING HORSES.

WE PITCH OUR TENTS IN LAKE PARK ON THE SHORES OF LAKE ATWOOD, THE LITTLE LAKE THE TOWN IS KNOWN FOR. THE ONLY THING THAT'S MISSING IS THE LAKE. THE LOCAL LIBRARIAN TELLS US THE LAKE DRIED UP DURING A DROUGHT. "BEEN GOING ON 6 YEARS," SHE TELLS US. THE LIBRARIAN'S FRIEND NODS.

"EVERYONE'S IN A GOOD MOOD WHEN THERE'S A LAKE," SHE SAYS.

10/05/06

I WAKE UP IN MY OWN TENT-SIZED RAINFOREST. THIS TENT I BORROWED FROM NICOLE BACK IN DETROIT (WHEN WAS THAT? A HUNDRED YEARS AGO?) HAS BEEN A FAITHFUL FRIEND. BUT WHEN THE DEW POINT RISES, IT CAN GET WET IN THERE. AS LITTLE DROPS OF COLD WATER PLOP ON MY FACE, I REMEMBER THE TIME I VISITED BIOSPHERE 2 WITH SARAH. THE BIOSPHERE WAS A GIANT TERRARIUM THAT A TEXAS BILLIONAIRE BUILT IN THE ARIZONA DESERT SOME YEARS AGO. IT WAS SUPPOSED TO BE A SELF-SUSTAINING CLOSED SYSTEM WHERE SCIENTISTS COULD STUDY CLIMATE AND ECOLOGY, BUT THEN EVERYTHING WENT WRONG — THE PIGS RAIDED THE VEGETABLE GARDEN, THE BEES DIED, AND FINALLY, THE OXYGEN RAN OUT AND THEY HAD TO OPEN THE WINDOWS. COMPARED TO THAT, NICOLE'S TENT

HAS PERFORMED PRETTY WELL.

IT'S A LOUSY MORNING, GREY AND CHILLY. I HANG MY TENT TO DRY, BUT IT'S USELESS. NONE OF US WANTS TO BIKE IN WEATHER LIKE THIS, SO WE SPEND THE MORNING KILLING TIME. HANGING OUT AT THE LIBRARY. CHECKING EMAIL. BROWSING THROUGH THE LOCAL MUSEUM WITH ITS VICTORIAN PERIOD ROOMS AND ITS PHOTOS OF THE ATWOOD HIGH SCHOOL MARCHING BAND IN NEW YORK FOR THE 1964 WORLD'S FAIR — WIDE-EYED KANSAS FARM KIDS IN THE FOREGROUND AND THE WORLD OF TOMORROW BEHIND. WHEN I STARTED THIS RIDE, I'D HOPED TO GO CLEAR ACROSS COUNTRY AND RIDE TRIUMPHANTLY ACROSS THE GOLDEN GATE BRIDGE INTO SAN FRANCISCO. BUT THERE'S SNOW UP IN THE ROCKIES NOW, AND I

REALIZE I'M GOING TO HAVE TO CALL IT QUITS.

LJR'S KNEE WAS BUGGING HER FOR A FEW DAYS. BUT NOW IT'S BETTER. SHE DARTS AHEAD OF MIKE AND ME AND PRETTY SOON, SHE'S BARELY VISIBLE. SEEING HER LIKE THAT, A LITTLE BLACK DOT UNDER A HUGE KANSAS SKY, MAKES ME FEEL LIKE A LITTLE BLACK DOT, TOO: SMALL AND LONELY AND LOST IN SPACE. MIKE PULLS UP CLOSE BEHIND ME.
"WHERE IS LJR GOING?" HE ASKS.
I SHRUG.

HIGHWAY 36 IS A GOOD ROAD FOR CYCLING. THE ONLY PROBLEM IS THE TRUCKS, THAT SCREAM PAST LIKE THE ANGEL OF DEATH; BIG RIG DRIVERS HAULING CATTLE OR WHEAT OR GASOLINE, HALF-CRAZY ON MICROWAVE BURRITOS AND

TRUCKER SPEED. SOME OF THE DRIVERS WAVE, AND SOME OF THEM WANT TO SMEAR US ACROSS THE HIGHWAY.

WE STOP AT A SODA FOUNTAIN IN TINY BIRD CITY. IT'S GETTING LATE, SO I ASK THE GIRL AT THE REGISTER IF THERE'S ANY PLACE IN TOWN TO STAY THE NIGHT. SHE SHRUGS.

"I GUESS YOU COULD CAMP IN ONE OF THE VACANT LOTS," SHE SAYS, WHICH IS A REASONABLE THING TO SUGGEST WHEN YOUR WHOLE TOWN IS TURNING INTO VACANT LOTS.

LJR WANTS TO STICK AROUND AT THE SODA FOUNTAIN AND GET A CHOCOLATE MALT. I WANT TO RIDE TO THE NEXT TOWN UP THE HIGHWAY BEFORE IT GETS DARK. WE GO BACK AND FORTH FOR A BIT. "OKAY, I'LL MEET YOU IN

ST. FRANCIS," I SAY. THEN I LEAVE.

I RIDE ALONE ON ONE OF THOSE RARE EVENINGS WHEN ALL THE CONDITIONS ARE RIGHT FOR A RIDE: BLUE SKIES, A STIFF TAIL WIND, AND FLAT TERRAIN — FLAT AND WIDE OPEN. A LANDSCAPE WITHOUT ANY SECRETS; WITHOUT A SINGLE THING TO HIDE. I ROLL UP TO A CONVENIENCE STORE ON THE EDGE OF ST. FRANCIS. THE LADY AT THE COUNTER SAYS THE EMPIRE MOTEL IS THE ONLY DECENT PLACE TO STAY IN TOWN — OR MAYBE SHE SAYS IT'S THE ONLY PLACE FOR DECENT PEOPLE TO STAY. A NICE YOUNG COUPLE BOUGHT THE MOTEL LAST YEAR AND HAVE BEEN FIXING IT UP. THE HUSBAND TELLS ME HE RESTORED THE NEON SIGN OUT FRONT SO IT LOOKS

THE SAME AS IT DID IN 1952: EMPIRE MOTEL – AIR CONDITIONING – VACANCY. "THE ONLY THING I ADDED IS THE WI-FI SIGN," HE SAYS.

LJR AND MIKE SHOW UP AN HOUR LATER. AFTER EVERYONE IS ASLEEP, I SNEAK OUT INTO THE PARKING LOT. THE OWNER OF THE MOTEL HAS SLIPPED WHITE SHEETS OVER A COUPLE LAMP POSTS, TURNING THEM INTO HALLOWEEN GHOSTS. WHEN THE WIND GUSTS, THE GHOSTS BILLOW UP LIKE THEY'VE TAKEN A DEEP BREATH THAT THEY HOLD FOR A WHILE THEN QUIETLY EXHALE.

10/06/06

THE WIND IS BLOWING HARD THIS MORNING, PICKING UP THE DUST AND WHIPPING THE FALLEN LEAVES

INTO LITTLE TORNADOS. LJR AND I WALK OVER TO THE DUSTY FARMER FOR COFFEE. THE GUY WHO OWNS OUR MOTEL TOLD US THAT THE GUY WHO OWNS THE DUSTY FARMER IS A JERK WHO LIKES TO MAKE TROUBLE, SO WE DECIDE TO CHECK THE PLACE OUT. THE COFFEE IS BAD AND THE PLACE IS A WRECK— A COBWEBBY TIME CAPSULE FROM THE 1960'S. WHEN AN OLD COUPLE COMES IN FOR BREAKFAST, THE OWNER HAS TO RUN ACROSS THE STREET TO A CONVENIENCE STORE TO BUY GROCERIES. IT'S DEPRESSING: THIS SAD OLD DINER, AND THE END OF THE BIKE TRIP, AND THE WEIRD AWKWARDNESS BETWEEN LJR AND ME.

WE SPEND THE DAY IN ST. FRANCIS WAITING FOR KYLE TO DRIVE OUT FROM DENVER TO PICK US UP.

I LEAF THROUGH AN ISSUE OF THE ST. FRANCIS HERALD. THERE'S AN ARTICLE ABOUT A GUY WHO HAS BEEN JOGGING ACROSS AMERICA. HE PASSED THROUGH TOWN A WEEK EARLIER, AND THE NEWSPAPER DID A WRITE-UP.

"HEY, LET'S GO TO THE NEWSPAPER OFFICE," I PROPOSE. MIKE AND LJR AGREE. SO WE HOP ON OUR BIKES AND RIDE DOWNTOWN.

THE EDITOR OF THE HERALD POLITELY TAKES NOTES WHILE WE TELL HER ABOUT OUR TRIP. SHE EVEN SNAPS A PHOTO OF US AS WE RIDE AWAY ON OUR BIKES.

OVER THE NEXT FEW WEEKS, I KEEP CHECKING THE NEWSPAPER'S WEB SITE FOR AN ARTICLE, BUT NOTHING EVER SHOWS UP. I CONSIDER WRITING AN IRATE

LETTER TO THE EDITOR UNTIL LJR POINTS OUT THAT THAT WOULD BE, YOU KNOW, PATHETIC.

KYLE SHOWS UP AT THE MOTEL AT 1 AM IN A BIG BUICK RENDEZVOUS THAT HE RENTED IN DENVER. THEN WE SIT AROUND TILL DAWN DRINKING BEER AND TELLING KYLE OUR BIKE STORIES. MOST PEOPLE WHO ASK YOU ABOUT A TRIP YOU TOOK ARE JUST BEING POLITE AND DEFINITELY DON'T WANT TO HEAR ALL THE GORY DETAILS, BUT KYLE WANTS TO KNOW EVERYTHING: WHERE WE SLEPT, AND WHERE WE ATE, AND HOW MANY DOGS CHASED US. HE WANTS TO HEAR ABOUT THE GUNSHOTS MIKE AND I HEARD ON CHOUTEAU ISLAND, AND HE WANTS TO KNOW WHY JEFF THE GUY IN

OHIO WHO LET US CAMP IN HIS BACK YARD DIDN'T CALL HIS WIFE FIRST TO SEE IF SHE WOULD MIND.

10/07/06

ST. FRANCIS, KANSAS IS JUST 14 MILES FROM THE COLORADO STATE LINE. IN THE MORNING, WE ASK KYLE IF IT'D BE OKAY IF WE RIDE TO THE BORDER, JUST SO WE CAN SAY WE MADE IT TO COLORADO. KYLE DOESN'T MIND AT ALL. THE WIND, HOWEVER, IS DEAD SET AGAINST THE PLAN.

HALFWAY TO THE STATE LINE, A BIG GUST KNOCKS MIKE OFF THE ROAD AND INTO THE GRASS. BY THE TIME I REACH HIM, HIS BACK TIRE IS ALREADY SOFT. I LOOK AT MIKE. HIS EYES ARE BLOODSHOT AND THERE'S A FLECK OF SPIT ON THE SIDE OF HIS MOUTH.

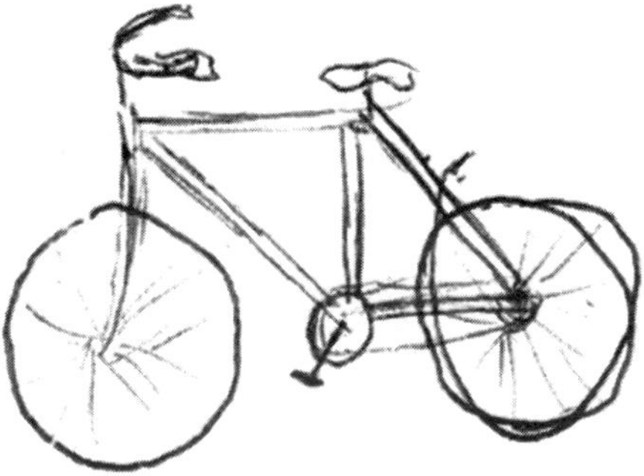

BIKE BY MIKE

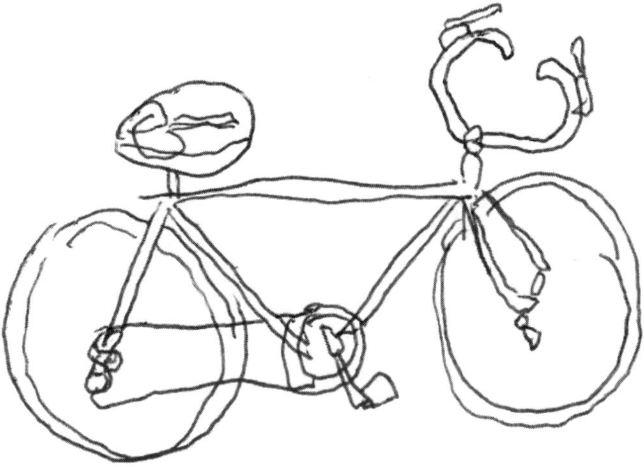

BIKE BY BILL

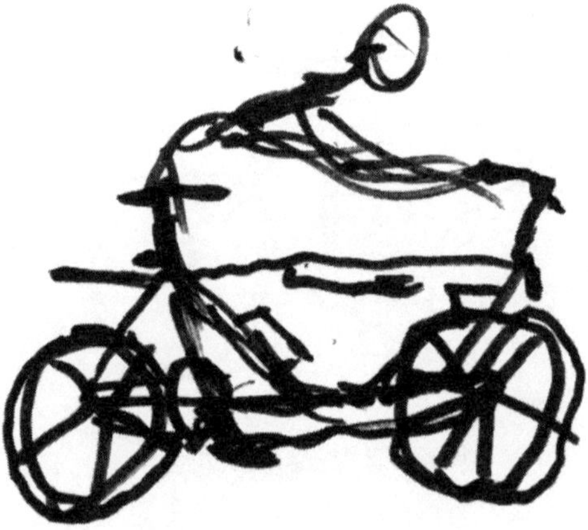

BIKE BY KYLE

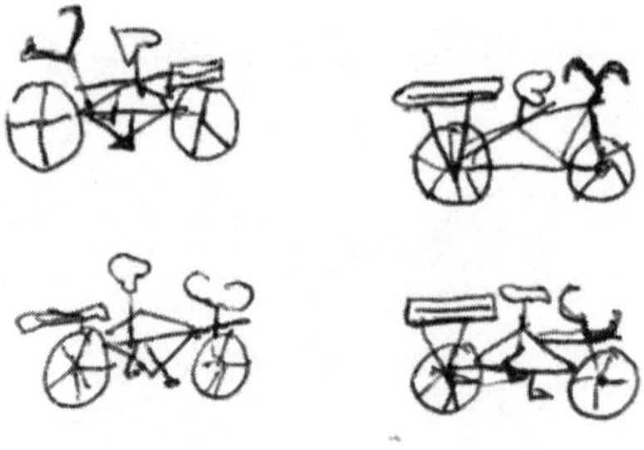

BIKE BY LJR

"GOAT HEAD," HE RASPS.

WE STRUGGLE ON. A COUPLE MILES FROM THE STATE LINE, WE SEE A CAR PARKED ON THE SHOULDER UP AHEAD. A COUPLE IS STANDING NEXT TO IT. THE GUY WAVES US DOWN. ON THE HOOD OF THE CAR, THERE'S A TUPPERWARE DISH FULL OF SLICED APPLES AND ANOTHER FULL OF DRIED FRUIT. THE GUY HANDS EACH OF US A PAPER CUP OF COLD WATER.

"WE SAW Y'ALL RIDING INTO THE WIND AND FIGURED YOU COULD USE A SAG STOP," HE SAYS, USING THE CYCLIST TERM FOR A REFRESHMENT BREAK. THE GUY TELLS US ABOUT A FEW OF HIS OWN LONG DISTANCE BIKE RIDES. THEN HE AND HIS WIFE WISH US LUCK AND DRIVE AWAY.

AT THE STATE LINE, THE SIGN THAT SAYS "WELCOME TO COLORFUL COLORADO" HAS BEEN KNOCKED COCKEYED BY THE WIND. THERE'S NOT MUCH BETWEEN HERE AND DENVER. TUMBLEWEEDS. BUZZARDS AND DESPERADOS. IF YOU PLAN TO TAKE A RIDE OUT HERE, YOU BETTER PACK A SIX SHOOTER AND AN EXTRA BOTTLE OF WATER.

KYLE SHOWS UP IN THE BIG BUICK, JUST AS PLANNED. WE BREAK DOWN OUR BIKES AND CRAM EVERYTHING IN THE BACK. THEN WE STAND THERE, STARING AT THE STUFF.

"THAT'S IT?" KYLE ASKS.

"THAT'S IT," I SAY.

HALFWAY TO DENVER, ON A LONELY STRETCH OF HIGHWAY 36, THE LOW FUEL LIGHT TURNS ON. THIS

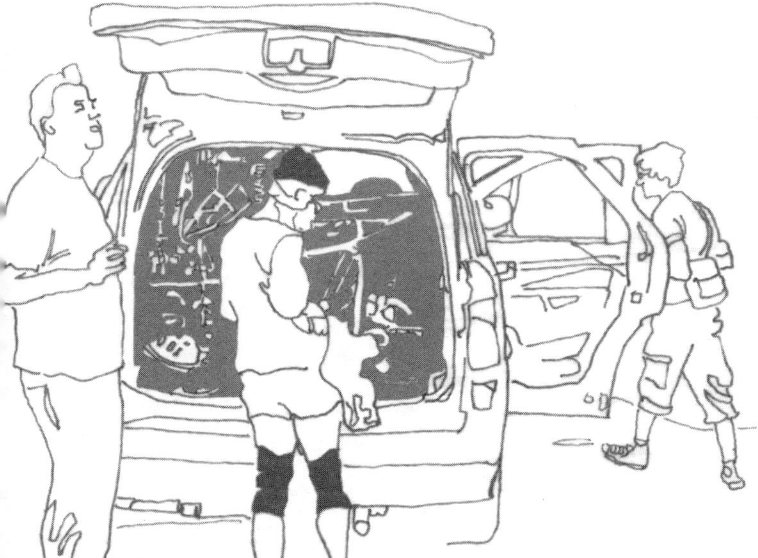

SHOULD MAKE ME NERVOUS, BUT NOT TODAY. TODAY IT FEELS LIKE A REPRIEVE. A LAST MINUTE CALL FROM THE GOVERNOR. MAYBE THE BIKE RIDE ISN'T OVER JUST YET.

WE RUN OUT OF GAS AT LAST CHANCE, COLORADO. THERE'S A BOARDED UP DAIRY QUEEN BUT NO GAS STATION. WE HIKE UP THE HIGHWAY AND FIND AN OLD GUY IN A BLAZE ORANGE JUMPSUIT WHO SELLS US A FEW GALLONS OF GAS FROM HIS PRIVATE STOCK IN THE GARAGE. "HAPPENS ALL THE TIME," HE TELLS US, A DEAD DEER STRUNG UP BEHIND HIM, DRIPPING BLOOD ON THE CEMENT FLOOR.

LONELY HIGHWAY 36 TURNS INTO

BUSY INTERSTATE 70, AND THEN WE'RE IN DENVER. KYLE LIVES IN A BASEMENT APARTMENT IN THE CAPITOL HILL NEIGHBORHOOD. WE MAKE HIM A THANK YOU DINNER: LJR'S TOFU PESTO PASTA, STEAMED ASPARAGUS, GARLIC BREAD, AND FRESH STRAWBERRIES WITH WHIPPED SOY CREAM FOR DESSERT. WHEN DINNER'S READY, WE PULL SOME MILK CRATES OUT ON THE SIDEWALK AND EAT RIGHT IN THE PATH OF THE SATURDAY NIGHT BAR CROWD.

10/08/06

AFTER BREAKFAST, LJR HEADS TO THE TRAIN STATION. IT'S HER SECOND GOODBYE OF THE TOUR, AND IT'S JUST AS SUDDEN AND UNEXPECTED AS THE LAST ONE.

MIKE AND I SPEND THE DAY PEDALING AROUND DENVER. WE DON'T SAY MUCH TO EACH OTHER. AFTER SPENDING EVERY MINUTE TOGETHER FOR THE LAST 800 MILES, I GUESS THERE'S NOTHING LEFT TO SAY.

WE VISIT THE DENVER ZINE LIBRARY. IT'S RUN BY A GUY NAMED KELLY. IT TURNS OUT KELLY IS AN ORGANIZATIONAL GENIUS WHO HAS BUILT AN ONLINE CATALOG OF THE WHOLE COLLECTION, ALL 7000 TITLES. ORGANIZING ZINES IS NO SMALL TASK, WHAT WITH THE NON-STANDARD SIZES AND IMPROVISATIONAL GRAMMAR AND THE OVERALL GENRE-FUCKING. MAYBE IT'S WRONG TO EVEN TRY. MAYBE ZINES SHOULD JUST BE TOSSED WILLY NILLY INTO MILK

CRATES, OR PILED HIGH ON THE BACK OF TOILETS. MAYBE THEY SHOULD JUST BE ORGANIZED ACCORDING TO THE SAME DUMB-LUCK LOGIC THAT ORDERS THE WHOLE UNIVERSE.

OUR LAST MOVIE SCREENING IS IN THE BASEMENT OF A LITTLE D.I.Y. BOUTIQUE CALLED THE FANCY TIGER THAT SELLS KNITTED SCARVES AND HANDMADE JEWELRY. THANKS TO KYLE, THE TURNOUT IS PRETTY GOOD: PUNK KIDS, KIDS FROM THE LOCAL BIKE PROJECT, KIDS FROM THE ZINE LIBRARY. ROAD KIDS AND ART KIDS AND CRUSTIES. THE MOVIE SCREEN IS A WRINKLY PLASTIC DROP CLOTH AND THE VIDEO PROJECTOR IS CROOKED.

MIKE SMILES AT ME ACROSS THE ROOM, AND I KNOW EXACTLY WHAT HE'S THINKING: THAT THIS IS THE PERFECT SHOW.

THEN IT'S OVER. WE STACK THE CHAIRS AND BOX UP THE ZINES, AND THE LITTLE MOVIE THEATER TURNS BACK INTO AN EMPTY BASEMENT. LATER, WE RIDE OVER TO A PUNK ROCK HOUSE CALLED THE VILLA VILLEKULLA, WHICH IS NAMED AFTER PIPPI LONGSTOCKING'S HOUSE. FOR DINNER, WE EAT DUMPSTERED CORN TORTILLAS AND THE LAST BACK YARD TOMATOES OF THE SEASON.

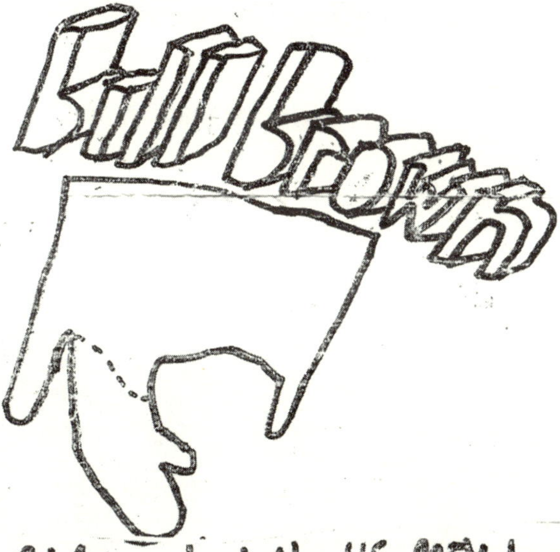

4 films about the US-MEX border

SUNDAY September 17 6pm

CREATIVE MINDS ART CENTER

3109 TROOST